GET OFF THE BUS

BY JOHN GODWIN

First published in Great Britain 2019

Published by P. J. Godwin

© P. J. Godwin

With thanks to Principal Bond Finance
Email: principalbondfinance@btopenworld.com

Thanks to Debbie Hunt and Kim Waldron
for their help in preparing the book
for publishing

Printed by
Kingfisher Print and Design, Totnes

ISBN: 978-1-9993563-0-9

Front cover photograph: Liam Garrison

GET OFF THE BUS

This book is dedicated to those that I love,
family and friends.

You know who you are.

A donation has been made in support of
WESC The West of England School and
College Foundation for youngsters
with visual impariment.

Content

Chapter 1

GET OFF THE BUS

YOU BOY!

"You boy, come to the front of the class".

Well we had all heard that before. A couple of times per week. Mr Lewis, our Form Teacher, would burst into life. His problem was that he was in the wrong career. He did not like children. He had been heard to say as much. I wonder if it came across in his teaching. What do you think? For sure.

His bored demeanor now changed dramatically. Here was his opportunity to perform. To get his kicks by producing his cane from the shelf behind his desk. To wield it around like an orchestra conductor's baton, Last Night of the Proms style before bringing it down full force onto a ten-year-old boy's outstretched palm.

I had never had the pleasure of joining in this performance first hand so to speak but had watched other boys take their punishment. Only ever the boys. It seemed that the girls were exempt. This early form of sexism implied that they never talked or played around in class. None of us wanted them included. It was interesting to watch the boys go forward. How would they take it? In the main, very well. The odd tear from fear before the cane or from genuine pain afterwards. Either way Mr Lewis was clearly enjoying the process too much. His eyes lit up and there was a leering slanted smile.

"Well! Are you coming boy?"

Hold it. He was looking at me!

" Hold out your hand Godwin, you have not been paying attention "

In my relaxed state I had not grasped reality. Clearly there had to be a mistake. My gran always said I was lovely, and my mother agreed. But yet, Mr Lewis was indeed looking directly at me. I knew there was no one behind me as I sat in the back row of the class. This was serious!

My ten-year-old brain was thinking the equivalent of what a bullying b*****d he is and does he not realise I may be ten now but one day I will be eighteen! Does he not realise what an error of judgment he is making? I had never liked him, and my inclination was proving well founded. At the front of the class the Lewis routine was in full flow. The cane was swishing in full rehearsal. Looking at him square in the eye I took the walk to the front of the class. Not exactly a prisoner taking his last walk of fresh air and freedom over the "Bridge of Sighs" in Venice before years in prison but you get my drift. Not pleasant.

"Hold out your hand Godwin, you have not been paying attention". With hindsight I should have said "That's because you are boring me. Your lack of interest in your job is evident and you appear frustrated. Any problems at home Mr Lewis?" But no such remark came forth. Out went the hand. An invitation but no RSVP.

Lewis wound himself up. His backswing would not have won praise in golfing circles. Too rushed and he did not keep his head still. The cane was coming down towards my vulnerable hand. My piano playing hand. I really mean my ex-piano playing hand.

My two-year period of piano lessons had recently concluded. Dad and I had mutually agreed it was not my thing following a Sunday tea visit from Auntie May and Uncle George. My two fingered rendition of Rule Britannia aborted half way through apparently did not represent value for money. The next day the piano was taken to the back garden where Dad literally took an axe to it. Not a man to mess around with! I digress.

The cane approached viciously. It was inches away when the hand almost with a will of its own withdrew. Timing is everything when withdrawing!! The cane now plunged out of control with no hand to stop it. The splitting sound as it hit the floor is still with me. "What have you done boy!" screamed Lewis clearly in shock. I have had this cane over 20 years dealing with boys like you!"

Well of course I had to hold my hand out again and he brought it down, but it was finished, broken and went in the bin. I went back to my desk in pain, but it felt in football terms as a good away draw. Very satisfying and my classmates had witnessed the retirement of the dreaded cane. I was a legend for five minutes!

Roll forward a few weeks. The headmaster of the school, he of flowing black robe and mortar board hat à la Batman made an announcement. He had accepted the challenge to play football against a much larger Swindon school who would travel to Calne to play us. We did not have a team but Mr Lewis was to organize and select one. Interesting. Several practice sessions found us with a team. It was not hard, we were football crazy anyway. Well most of us. One or two may have been press ganged into making the team. My brother Gary and I spent hours on our small driveway, one touch, two touch football practice and short games. We would later play for Calne Town Football Club together. We supported Swindon Town. More of that later.

Mr Lewis borrowed kit and the local youth club football pitch. The headmaster announced school would close for the afternoon match and the entire school, pupils and staff, would be marching to the ground to support the team.

Come the day of the match Lewis called us together. We were representing the school. The pupils, staff and ourselves. His reputation as a motivator was on the line. "No fighting, spitting or swearing boys! Keep your heads up and do us proud. No tactics except keep your positions and don't be pushed around". "We need a Captain" he said before throwing me the match ball. "You'll do Godwin. I know you have quick reactions!" Hold it, Lewis had cracked a joke. He was human after all!

The game came and went quickly. The Swindon boys who played regularly and had more boys to choose from won 4-1. We did well, and Lewis seemed satisfied. I scored our goal and will not forget the feeling as the ball hit the roof of the net and the noise as the school cheered. The rush of euphoria was great, and I wanted more of that for sure. The headmaster 'Batman' was pleased. Lewis said well played and good goal. In that single day he had cracked a joke, made me Captain and said well done. What a great guy, I had always liked him!!

The importance of sport was hitting me. It had brought the school together. There was a tangible feeling of community and family. The team pulling together as a unit. Taking on a challenge together. Character was being shown. Skills were coming through. Shortcomings were there but no matter. They could be worked on. The whole sport thing was lighting up in front of me.

This book explores many sporting experiences and life observations. It is a fond and hopefully humorous journey which you may relate to. Enjoy!

" . . .That's because you are boring me. Your lack of interest in your job is evident and you appear frustrated. Any problems at home Mr Lewis? **"**

Chapter 2

KEEP RUNNING FLASH

The youth club emptied early as a joker had dispensed a handful of stink bombs. It was unbearable!

Walking home in our early teens it had been snowing. For no apparent reason my school friend Flash on impulse made a snowball and threw it at a house. It hit the lounge window. What a plonker. Much to his surprise within seconds the front door burst open and a fairly fit and understandably angry man came running out intent on catching the culprit no doubt with retribution in mind. The chase was on!

Two things occurred to me. Firstly, the man who was now showing a good turn of pace would not know who had thrown the snowball. We were both in the frame. Not good. Secondly and much better news was that I could always outrun Flash so logically would not be the one to be caught. All that was required was to stay ahead of Flash.

We ran the first quarter of a mile in reasonable time. Past the Calne Bowling Green and ironically past the stone that had long stood in tribute to one of Calne's finest sons, Walter Goodall George 1858-1943. He ran a mile in four minutes 12 ¾ seconds in August 1886 a World record for 29 years. Flash was going to need a personal best as our man was gaining. Closing the gap.

"Keep running Flash" I encouraged keeping a healthy twenty yards ahead. Running downhill now past the vicarage which again was ironic as I suspect Flash was praying for help, divine intervention perhaps!

Right turn now along the path and bridge over Doctors Pond so named after Doctor J B Priestly who is credited with discovering oxygen in Wiltshire in 1774. He lived and worked at Bowood House near Calne where he was the librarian and scientific guru for Lord Shelbourne. Well Flash was clearly in need of oxygen and plenty of it. Would he need a doctor too? We kept running leaving the Mill House, later to be the home of the actor David Hemmings, well behind.

On and on, Flash was tiring badly but so was our chaser. Flash was never fit really. He had one good lung, the other was to require surgery a few years later. Our chance came when around a bend so out of sight we flew over a fence at the Catholic Church into Flash's garden, back door and sanctuary!

Ian Montague Fell was given the nickname Flash by me. When the local boys turned out for a game of football in jeans and trainers he would be the one with a new leather football and all gold Wolverhampton Wanderers kit. He was always tall, getting to his six feet four inches at an early age. He would run or lope down the right wing so Flash just seemed to fit. I am godfather to his daughter Josephine. Alex, his son, has followed family tradition and is a Swindon Town follower. Flash's father Monty rarely missed a match like all of us back then. He was a gifted drummer and when away from his office played with a jazz band. Flash kept that interest going and I well remember sitting behind the stage with him watching Buddy Rich perform in Bristol at the Colston Hall. Buddy was arguably the World's greatest ever drummer.

Flash, while sportingly not prolific, he was in fairness a top dog swimmer. But injury prone. Winning a school sprint in the pool we had raised money to build, he forgot to stop and swam into the end wall. No damage to the pool. Not so good for Flash's nose. Blood everywhere. Another time playing cricket for the school at Bradford on Avon Flash was warming up to go in to bat. The cricket ball flew off the bottom of the bat knocking his two front teeth clean out of his mouth. Two little stumps remained, poor chap. Dracula was showing in the local cinema and Flash was getting into character.

Another time it was a beautiful sunny day, so we decided to give Geography a miss. Instead we walked through the Geography room and out on to the flat sun roof hidden from view to take in a few rays and relax. The fire alarm went off for a practice drill, the door was locked. We were stuck on the roof watching the entire school pupils and staff assemble on the Tennis Courts below for roll call. One of our class mates saw us peering down and cleverly mimicked our names for us when called. Good boy but another close shave!

When GCSE 'O' level results came out I had a six-week holiday job as a dining hall porter at the Butlins Holiday Camp, Bognor Regis. A letter duly arrived from mother and my results were good. She reported that others including Ian Edwards and Pauline Dunn had done okay but that Flash had not got his yet! That was code for Flash having intercepted the results letter. He had done poorly and was not going to rush into breaking the news to his parents.

We went to Southsea for a few days break. Dad had thrown me the keys to his new and first car, a Morris Oxford. Very trusting especially as I had only recently learned to drive, I learnt with Mother and we took our driving tests on the same day in Chippenham. Two passes! Flash and I stayed in a little bed and breakfast. On leaving the landlady said, "Most guests leave me a tip boys". Flash told her to look on the dressing room table in the bedroom. "Hit the gas quickly Godwin" he smiled as we drove away!

Flash and I kind of stayed around our home town while others moved away to university or career paths. We would move ourselves but have kept in touch. At his wedding to Janet all was well until he waved and went to drive away on honeymoon. We had jacked his wheels up so the car would not move. He was not amused. We were! Years later he moved to Florida for a few years. He asked us to put him up for a weekend while his VISA arrived. It took two and a half months! More of Flash later particularly around golf and our coveted Golf Umbrella Trophy!

Chapter 3

GET OFF THE BUS

It is August 1967. I am sat on a bus near the front travelling the hundred miles or so from my home town of Calne in Wiltshire to London. My school friend Christopher Hall and I are just fifteen. His uncle has a butchers shop and nice house in London, so we are going up to stay for a week's holiday. Lovely. In those days travel was limited, not so easy as it is today. A school trip might be a train ride say to Cardiff Castle. We did that one time and I recall a rainy, wet day trudging around eating lots of chocolate and ice cream and then being distinctly unwell on the train back! Boyhood vices pass with time as we swap them. It's red wine and whisky now!

A family holiday would normally be a week in Southsea. No foreign travel but if the budget allowed we were off to Southsea on the South Coast for fun on the boating lake, crazy golf, the fairground and the ever-popular visit to see HMS Victory with all it's great history. People were smaller then in the 1700's and the low ceiling reflected that. The inside decks were painted red to mask the blood of the sailors in battle. Lord Horatio Nelson would wear his full dress uniform at sea and this left him vulnerable to the sniper's bullet that eventually got him at the Battle of Trafalgar.

Nelson had previously lost his right arm at the Battle of Santa Cruz, Tenerife during a famous career but it was victory at the Battle of Trafalgar against the combined fleets of the French and Spanish navies that cemented his place as a national hero.

On one early trip to Southsea aged around six I lost my little wallet complete with all my pocket money. A kindly lady at the hotel organized a collection which trebled what was lost. The generosity of folk! Should have tried that one again! I digress.

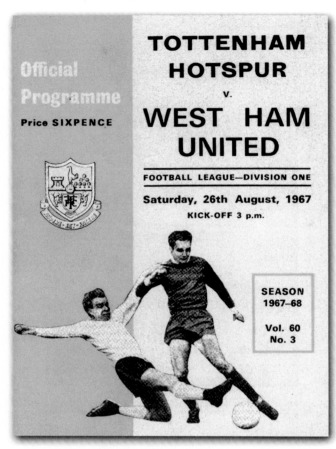

Official Programme

Price SIXPENCE

TOTTENHAM HOTSPUR

v.

WEST HAM UNITED

FOOTBALL LEAGUE—DIVISION ONE

Saturday, 26th August, 1967

KICK-OFF 3 p.m.

SEASON
1967–68

Vol. 60
No. 3

Back on the bus to London we reached the outskirts. Now it was proper London. Hussle and bustle. Stopping at traffic lights I looked out and on the path was a red/pink ten-shilling note. A lot of money in those days. People were walking past oblivious. I was out of my seat in a flash. "Open the door driver, I need to get off the bus". I jumped out and picked up the ten-shilling note. It felt like picking up say £50 in today's money. Great.

My joy turned to horror as I realised the lights had changed, and the bus was off without me. My friend, case and the bus had gone.

I was bright enough to know there were lots of butchers shops in London. Help! We were headed for Victoria Coach Station and I had ten shillings which would cover a taxi but to hell with losing my windfall. As luck would have it another bus with a Victoria Coach Station sign as its destination stopped at the lights. I knocked on the door, the driver took pity on my plight, laughed and said, "Jump on son".

We somehow arrived just ahead of the original bus and I was at Victoria to greet Chris. "How in the hell did you manage that" he cried.

The holiday went well apart from blowing a big bubble gum which collapsed onto my face. I had pre-shaving early facial stubble. Removing the gum left my face blotchy and red.

The highlight was Saturday 26th August 1967. 3 o'clock kick-off. Tottenham Hotspur v West Ham united.

We stood behind the goal. 55,831 attendance. This was starting a life-long trend. Any holiday is better including some top-class sport!

Spurs won 5-1. Two classic Jimmy Greaves goals including a one stride penalty passed just inside the post. Classic. More of Jimmy later. A bullet header from Cliff Jones. Wonderful. What an atmosphere at White Hart Lane. I was hooked.

Around five years later and I was going out with a lovely girl, Carole Dunn. I had been to school with Pauline, her sister, and funnily enough we had a couple of dates in a young first kiss, hold hands and what happens next innocent way. Anyway, Carole looked at me one night and said, "Do you remember getting off a bus in London?" "I was sat on that bus with my Dad. We were going to visit my grandfather who was a Chelsea Pensioner. We could not believe what you did. My Dad thought you were a complete prat. Funnily enough, now we have been going out for six months and he has got to know you, he still does!" Charming. When dropping Carole home, if we sat in the car too long Howard's head would appear looking over the hedge. It's okay Howard, with two daughters myself now, I get it!!

Fast forward to 5th July 2015. Déjà vu. Sat on a bus again. Nearly 50 years later but not really accepting the speedy age spurt. Call it denial, but I refuse, for example, to join the senior section at my golf club. Isn't that for older people? Candidates for knee and hip replacements. I will deal with the whole golf thing later based on 40 years of playing and experiences including the big one 'Golf Club Captain'.

This bus is in Canada. Vancouver City. I am with my wife Anne and our regular travelling companions Alan and Diane Yates. It's the city bus tour. Through Stanley Park over 1000 acres that border downtown Vancouver almost entirely surrounded by the waters of Vancouver Harbour and English Bay, named after Lord Stanley, the Governor General from Britain, and happy to continue our colonisation trends of naming places why after ourselves of course. How very British. Vancouver Park was too easy – let's call it Stanley Park because I have been here five minutes. Onwards past Burrard Street Bridge and False Creek. We have been to Canada Place on the waterfront with its cruise ship terminal, convention centre and hotels. Along Coal Harbour with its sea planes, cruise charters and Deadman's Island away in the distance.

A truly beautiful city, vibrant and busy. Historic but modern and alive.

Multi-cultural with a high number of Chinese, many from Hong Kong wanting to get out when power was handed to China in 1997. Historically they were second class only given the vote after fighting for Canada in the Second World War. The Chinese Exclusion Act was repealed. Seems reasonable. These city bus tours are always a good idea. You know the routine. A drive round to get the flavour and see the main sights. Our driver/guide announced a detour to avoid the crowds. It was 2.30 and just up the road with a 4pm kick-off at the BC Palace Stadium was the Ladies Soccer World Cup Final. It was a sell out with 50,000 people converging. USA v Japan. The streets were alive with stars and stripes of the USA mainly. Was I, as a sports nut, going to drive past a World Cup Final without trying to get in? What do you think? Stop the bus! The driver braked sharply. A quick "See you later back at the hotel" to my wife, Diane and Alan and I was off the bus into the thronging mass of people. The stadium was visible down a sloping road not far away. Let's go.

I spotted a Canadian guy who wanted to offload a couple of tickets talking to a tout who was far from happy when I thrust some dollars forward and almost grabbed a ticket. "You can't do that buster" the tout shouted. "Can and have my friend" I declared before hot footing it into the crowd. Have a nice day! I was in! More of the game and Canada later.

Chapter 4

SECONDARY OR GRAMMAR

People have debated Grammar Schools and Secondary Schools for decades. Is it right to choose at eleven what potential a child has? To decide how clever they are or could be? Guess what, I went to both! I want to tell you a little story.

Back when I was eleven there was a Grammar School examination procedure. Exam one, a test. I passed. Exam two, a more difficult test, I passed. Many of my friends and classmates were now destined for Secondary School. The rest of us faced a ten minute interview with the Grammar School Headmaster, Mr Tickner.

My parents were pleased. My Dad had a difficult childhood. He had served his country for five years in and after the Second World War. A tank driver mainly in the middle East. On returning to his home town of Calne he vowed in his early 20's never to leave. The war and being away affected everyone. All he wanted was to succeed in his work and to raise his family. He married "Miss Calne" my mother Desna. Johnny was content. He wanted the best for his children above all else. My brother Gary and I wanted for nothing. He was the governor but a softie really. My sisters Julie and Rebecca arrived much later when we were teenagers.

Dad wanted to take no chances. He bought a nice suit for me, collar and tie. I was bright enough, I liked my sport and, in all fairness, knew I was as good academically as the rest. A ten minute interview and a few weeks later a letter through the post. I had failed the interview with Mr Tickner and was, at eleven, therefore a failure destined for Secondary School. Tickner was not to know then that this was the same failure who would arrive at his school, Calne Bentley Grammar School, one year later going on to gain O and A levels, star in school plays, Captain his soccer team to the County final and play for Wiltshire at Soccer. The same boy who regularly would have to knock on his door pre-assembly with sports results as Captain for him to read out at assembly.

I never mentioned the interview at eleven plus but hey, I bet we both remembered. I never got to be Head Boy or deputy but guess what, his son Edmond Tickner did!

Now the Godwin's do not brood or bear a grudge. Not much! My father was outraged and was not taking this travesty without a fight. Good man. He visited Tickner to discuss the situation man to man. A fly on the wall I would like to have been!! Tickner was probably never the same man again.

Over the next few months Dad visited Tickner again a bit like an Italian Godfather perhaps making an offer he could not refuse. More importantly he visited the Secondary School Head, Mr Springate. Now he was a jovial man's man. He understood exactly and they empathized. They set up another end of year test and guess what, I passed! Mr Springate did the interview and while I was now off to Grammar School it would not surprise me if Mr Springate and Dad were off for a pint.

A footnote here. I was not the star pupil in the A stream at Secondary. I left behind half of the class who were ahead of me in first year results but whose Dad had not made their case. Food for thought. At Grammar I more than held my own but am in a first-hand position to tell you that the top boys and girls at Secondary could easily swop with the bottom at Grammar.

The standards at Grammar were higher. Better teachers, less problem kids, more ambition. Perhaps we should aim at the highest standards for all. We cannot hold back our brightest by putting them in with the obviously less capable. It's the middle tier that concern me. The ones who failed an eleven plus pantomime exam and who missed out because they did not have a Dad like mine who cared enough not to take it lying down. Well played John Godwin Senior, and thank you.

Chapter 5

STUCK IN A FIELD

1066, Battle of Hastings. King Harold, son of Godwin, was in a field trying to stop William of Normandy otherwise known as William the Conqueror from invading England. King Harold (Godwin) had posted his men behind a strong palisade, a fence made of posts driven into the ground. William, finding he could not get through, ordered his left wing to turn and fly. The English unwisely chased them only for the Normans to turn with such fury that the English were slain or scattered in all directions. Harold surrounded by a few thousand of his brave retainers maintained the fight until Harold famously took an arrow in his eye and fell lifeless to the ground.

Roll on 900 years and another son of Godwin, yours truly, is in a field with problems of his own.

It is 30th July 1966, the day of the World Cup Final at Wembley. England v West Germany. The problems, in essence, are:

1.	I have been forced to be in the Boy Scouts now for several years, do not enjoy being under canvas and would prefer to be playing sport anything but scouting despite my father's insistence it was character forming and good for you. Really!
2.	We are attending a World Scout Jamboree at Ogborne St George near Marlborough only 15 miles from Calne. Scouts have travelled from all over the World.
3.	It has rained all week to the extent some tents are flooded out and boys moved to wooden huts.

4. My father, bless him, has agreed to pick me up to pop back for the final on TV. He has clearly changed him mind later telling me it was only fair the boys stuck together. Quarter of an hour before kick-off I realised he was not coming.

Like all good scouts, you have to adapt. Their motto is BE PREPARED. Well I was not prepared for this nightmare. Except we had a radio and so did most tents. The boys huddled together in the cold and rain. When the Germans scored first a distant cheer went up clearly from the German tent. But, and of course it's history, we won 4-2 with goals from Martin Peters and a Geoff Hurst hat trick. Wonderful.

Alf Ramsey's England were World Cup Winners for the one and only time and fifty years later we have not matched it by winning. It was historic. I was stuck in a field. I suppose it was still an event in its own way. The boys cheering as Banks, Cohen, Wilson, Moore, Charlton J, Stiles, Peters, Charlton B, Hunt, Ball and Hurst got the job done. The cheers around the camp, mostly for England.

The final is remembered for the Hurst hat trick, the only one in a World Cup Final. Did the ball cross the line for the second of his goals? Well, I was listening on the radio with no view at all but as an Englishman of course it was over the line! The linesman who gave the goal was Tofiq Bharamov from Azerbaijan in the USSR. He promised he had not been influenced by Russia losing to West Germany nor by the Second World War although one story exists that when asked why he gave the goal he simply said, "Stalingrad"!!

Hurst's third goal in the final minute made it 4-2 to England. The goal gave rise to one of the most famous sayings in English football BBC commentator Kenneth Wolstenholme described as follows

"And here comes Hurst. He's got …. some people are on the pitch. They think it's all over. It is now! It's four".

In fairness to scouting I am sure it's good if you like waking up in a wet, cold field rather than your own bed. It's great if you enjoy sitting around the camp fire with in some cases half wits waiting for your under-cooked sausage. In Calne, to get to the Scout Hall, you walked past the mods and rockers with their motorbikes and micky takes in your nice Scout uniform and large floppy hat.

It's great if you want to learn all sorts of knots, (in fairness, the reef knot is useful for joining string or rope), it's good if you want to earn badges for your uniform for all manner of trivia. My respect to Scout Masters who give up their time and help youngsters to get a life. I already had one. The moral here could be not to force kids to do something they have an inherent dislike of. Let them do things they want to throw themselves into and enjoy. Here endeth the lesson!

" And here comes Hurst. He's got ….
some people are on the pitch. They
think it's all over. It is now! It's four. "

Chapter 6

HANDS ON
THE LEAGUE CUP

1969. So it's another school assembly at the Calne Bentley Grammar School. The usual routine with the entire school packed into the hall. The teachers sat on the stage and the Headmaster would enter at the back of the hall in his robes and black mortar board hat. The school would rise in respect and ceremony. A few announcements, orders for the day, match results. A prayer, a hymn and then all file out for lessons. Riveting.

Calne Bentley Grammar 1st XI Soccer Team 1971. I've got the ball.

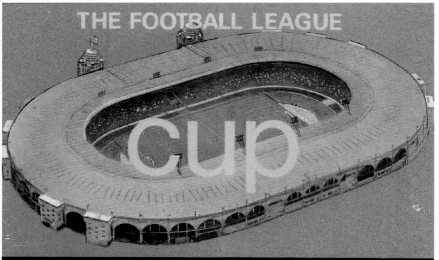

THE FOOTBALL LEAGUE
cup

ARSENAL v SWINDON TOWN

Saturday
March 15
1969

Kick
Off
3.30p.m.

final

OFFICIAL PROGRAMME TWO SHILLINGS
Incorporating Special Issue of Football League Review

THE EMPIRE STADIUM — WEMBLEY

THE FOOTBALL LEAGUE

CUP FINAL

SAT., MARCH 15, 1969

KICK-OFF 3.30 p.m.
YOU ARE ADVISED TO TAKE UP
YOUR POSITION BY 3 p.m.

J.S.Lie CHAIRMAN
WEMBLEY STADIUM LTD

NORTH TERRACE
25/–

TO BE RETAINED

(SEE PLAN AND CONDITIONS ON BACK)

TURNSTILES
D
ENTRANCE
3
ROW
6
SEAT
265

But not today. We had guests. Football guests. Swindon Town had defied all the odds. The 3rd division team had won the League Cup beating mighty Arsenal 3-1 at Wembley. The County of Wiltshire was proud. The country was stunned.

Mr Tickner spoke of the achievement and from the wings of the stage on cue from the Head's introduction walked on the Swindon Town Captain, Stan Harland. A strong, tall, number 6 central defender. Steadfast leader and inspirational. Good in the air and sound on the ground. With Roger Smart, a hard working born and bred in Swindon inside forward who had scored the first goal at Wembley.

You can imagine the excitement as they held the cup aloft to the rapturous applause of the entire school. Mr Tickner then made an announcement which I had no idea was coming. "As a token of our admiration and thank you for coming to the school today I invite you to go to lunch with our school football manager. Mathematics teacher John Williams and our school first team football captain "....". Blimey, that would be me then!

And so, an hour or two later, I found myself in Jonny Williams car sat in the back with Roger Smart complete with the League Cup on my lap. We headed for the George Inn, Sandy Lane near Calne a lovely old pub renowned for its Wadworths 6X ale and its good food. The Wadworths Brewery is at Devizes around 6 miles away. They still use the huge dray horses to deliver kegs locally. I have a limited edition print hanging in my dining room which I admired of the dray horses in action. It was sold to me having hung on the wall at the neighbouring Lansdowne Arms, scene of my 21st birthday party.

The meal at the George was of course a thrill. The League Cup sat on the table much to the excitement of the customers and staff. The pub was run by Mr and Mrs Endress whose daughter Jackie was at school with me. She married Kevin, also from our class, and became Jackie Knowles. We have kept in touch for over 50 years and we have in 2015 visited her in South Africa where she has been for over 30 years.

My memory of the meal was that Stan Harland, a typical scouser from Liverpool, never stopped talking! Roger, Jonny and I couldn't get a word in. To hear firsthand about the cup run, Wembley, Swindon Town, the players, it was a young boy's dream. The steak compared favourably to school dinners also!

ROYAL ALBERT HALL

Manager : C. B. Hopper   Doors Open 6.30 p.m.   Commence 7.30 p.m.   Matchmaker : MICKEY DUFF

TUESDAY, 9th MARCH, 1965

MIKE BARRETT presents INTERNATIONAL BOXING

The 'K.O. SPECIALIST' v The 'IRON MAN'

10 (3 min.) RDS. INTERNATIONAL MIDDLEWEIGHT CONTEST AT 11st. 8lbs.

RUBIN (HURRICANE)   HARRY

CARTER v SCOTT

(New Jersey, U.S.A.). Contender for World's Title. Considered the most colourful fighter in the World. K.O'd. Emile Griffith, 1 rd., Florentino Fernandez, 1 rd.

(Bootle). Central Area Champion. The toughest man in Britain today. Fought great fights with Laszlo Papp, Gert van Heerden, etc. Has never been floored.

10 (3 min.) RDS. INTERNATIONAL LIGHTWEIGHT CONTESTS AT 9st. 12lbs.

JOE (OLD BONES)   VIC

BROWN v ANDREETTI

(Texas, U.S.A.). Former Lightweight Champion of the World. Currently in great form. Won his last five contests.

(Hoxton). Now ready to box for the British Title. Last two contests defeated Joe Tetteh and World rated Rafiu King.

10 (3 min.) RDS. FEATHERWEIGHT CONTEST AT 9st. 2lbs.

LENNIE (THE LION)   JOHNNY

WILLIAMS v MANTLE

(Maesteg). Making a welcome return here. Only lost to Frankie Taylor in 34 fights.

(Battersea). London's outstanding Featherweight. Just K.O'd. Con Mount Bassey in 1 rd.

8 (3 min.) RDS. WELTERWEIGHT CONTEST AT 10st. 9lbs.

RALPH   IVAN

CHARLES v WHITER

(West Ham). Undefeated to date.

(Battersea). A crowd-pleasing young prospect.

SUPPORTING CONTESTS WILL FEATURE BRIAN BRAZIER, DENNIS PLEACE AND THE PROFESSIONAL DEBUT OF BRIAN PACKER

TICKETS £6.6.0   £4.4.0   £3   30/-   15/-

Tickets from: MIKE BARRETT PROMOTIONS, BOX OFFICE—OPEN 9 a.m.-11 p.m. 7 DAYS A WEEK—(Frank Goldberg) 38 Rosebery Road, S.W.2, TUL. 6019 and TUL. 1478. Royal Albert Hall, KEN 8212. Archie Kasler, LEY 7844. Al Phillips, BIS 1373. Alf Mancini, REV 6502. Len Mancini, REN 4501. Butchers Arms, York Way, NOR 4532. Thomas A'Beckett Gym, ROD 7334. The Colleen Bawn, 6ER 3842. Cambridge Gymnasium, 9 Earlham Street, W.C.2. Usual Agents.

Alfred Robins & Co. Ltd. (T.U.) 4/6 Wilkes Street, London, E.1 — 825 7521

Chapter 7

ITS IN THE BLOOD AND 1969

Growing up sport was always there. In March 1965 Dad took brother Gary and I to London for a cultural visit. In particular he wanted us to see a bridge and a hall. Well the bridge turned out to be Stamford Bridge to see Chelsea beat Spurs 3-1. The hall turned out to be the Albert Hall for a top boxing tournament. We may have visited a museum or two but it's the sport I remember.

Part of the sporting scene and very much integral to our way of life like so many families was the local football team. In our case, it was Swindon Town. We rarely missed a game and stood in the Town End to the side of the goal around the edge of the penalty box halfway back.

Those games were great, especially the evening games under floodlights. The same people would tend to head for their space and the atmosphere was electric. The same guys would give the same players plenty of stick. Harold Feltham for example a friend of Dad's, had a dislike for Keith Morgan, a right half, and would give him stick even in the warm up. Actually, he could play, but Harold had made his mind up. As for referee's, well, they had no chance.

We had Mike Summerbee, a fast and aggressive winger who went on to fame with Manchester City and England. Ernie Hunt, a bandy legged inside forward who ended up playing for Everton and Wolves. Over the years, teams came and went. Good seasons, not so good seasons. But no season like 1969.

We had a good team. The stand out star and the best player I have ever seen was Don Rogers. Now bear in mind I've seen a lot of great players all Internationals and so on. But I stick with my statement and it is a sentiment shared by plenty of others mainly Swindon Town supporters but also by one or two Crystal Palace fans where he

John Trollope MBE, Jensen and Don Rogers at Wembley

spent some time including scoring a match of the day goal of the season. He played for England Under 23 alongside big names. He played for England B and starred and scored. It borders on criminal that when in his prime he did not go to a top club or to the 1970 World Cup Finals in Mexico. For Swindon Town it was good news.

When Don Rogers got the ball there was a buzz around the ground. When he set off on a run you could feel the anticipation. Don was quick, had great balance and a body swerve that sent opponents the wrong way. He played approaching 500 games for Swindon with 181 goals. Not bad for a left wing. In fairness he moved inside a lot. He had a great understanding with John Trollope MBE and our left back. His tough tackling and overlapping with Don was telepathic. John played 770 league games for Swindon a record number of appearances for one club. He served Swindon in different roles for 40 years. Both Don and John are legends. Imagine my great joy last year when I took my grandson to Wembley to see Swindon Town in a play-off final. Jensen and I parked the car and Don and John were parked next to us. We had a chat. I told them "I wish you boys were playing today". In unison they replied, "So do we".

So that is why I have on my office wall this great picture of Jensen stood between Don Rogers and John Trollope at Wembley. Jensen was not sure who they were. He knows now after watching footage with me. Wow!

So, 1969 saw Swindon Town, a third division team, get to the League Cup Final at Wembley against the mighty Arsenal. They worked hard to get there with some good wins including a semi-final win over Burnley at the Hawthorns, home of West Bromwich Albion. We went up by coach and stood behind a goal towards the edge of the penalty area. Sort of Right Back territory. The game had everything and if forced to pick the best game I have seen this one would be right up there.

At 2-2 Peter Noble took the ball on his chest just inside the penalty area. He produced a spectacular volley which hit the roof of the net right in front of us. Rapture for us, desolation for Burnley. Peter later played for Burnley and ended up with a fruit and vegetable shop up there. Swindon Town were going to Wembley as huge underdogs but hey, we had a great team and we had Don Rogers. It was hard luck for Burnley as I am always happy to discuss with Michael Cook, a former Burnley season ticket holder now living in Teignmouth.

Come the day of the match it seemed as if the whole of Wiltshire was on the M4. With Dad at the wheel, Mother, Gary and I were en route. The red of Swindon adorned cars and coaches as we set off in hope and anticipation. We had a strong side.

		DOWNSBOROUGH		
2	5	6	3	
Thomas	Burrows	Harland (Captain)	Trollope	
	9	4		
	Smith	Butler		
7	8	10	11	
Heath	Smart	Noble	Rogers	

" How can you leave a player like
Don out of the England side?
He's fantastic. **"**

Peter Downsborough in goal, a little on the short side for a goalie but safe and a good shot stopper. A good strong defence. Rod Thomas at right back. Good tackler and Welsh International destined for glory at Derby County. The ever-dependable John Trollope at left back. Stan Harland and Frank Burrows, pillars in the centre of defence. In midfield Joe Butler, a good link man. John Smith who looked overweight but who added a touch of class. Don Heath, a pacey right winger. Peter Noble and Roger Smart up front. Not big but both industrious together. Don Rogers on the left and ever dangerous.

The Horse of the Year show had been allowed to be held at Wembley earlier in the week and so the pitch was not as good as you would have expected for the home of football. The 'Don' showed his class with some clever early runs. Arsenal knew they had a game on their hands. Red hot favourites but the teams looked evenly matched. Roger Smart put Swindon ahead with a scrappy goal.

Shortly after the goal something was burning. We could all smell it. That was the first clue. The second clue was when wisps of smoke started to waft from Dad's coat. In the excitement a guy behind had dropped his cigarette into Dad's coat hood. This was the era before smoking was banned. The smouldering coat was extinguished. So what? We were ahead!

Bobby Gould, the Arsenal centre forward, equalized near the end of the match. I saw him a few years ago in Teignmouth Golf Club. He was not crying as he did at Wembley. The emotion got to him on equalizing. Understandable or was he injured? His autobiography was a good read.

Into extra time and after some good saves from Peter Downsborough Don Rogers poked Swindon ahead from a corner kick.

With time running out Roger Smart played a nice pass putting Don Rogers clear just into the Arsenal half. Time stood still as he bore down on the Arsenal goal. No-one would catch him with his pace. Only Bob Wilson in the Arsenal goal could save them. Wilson ran out and the 'Don' shimmied his hips and dropped his shoulder. Don was around him with ease before passing into the empty net. 3-1 game over. History.

Don Rogers turned and strolled back to the half way line. The coolest man in the stadium. Best player I've ever seen.

Just for fun here is my best Swindon Town team. The only criteria is that I had to see them play. One notable omission would be the Spurs legend Dave Mackay. He was past his sell by date when he joined us and committed the unforgivable when he took over as Manager. He sold Don Rogers!

P DOWNSBOROUGH

2	5	6	3
R Thomas	F Burrows	S Harland (Captain)	J Trollope

4
S McMahon

8	10
E Hunt	G Hoddle

7	9	11
M Summerbee	D Shearer	D Rogers

Same again, my best England team and I had to see them play.

G BANKS

2	5	6	3
G Neville	T Adams	B Moore (Captain)	S Pearce

4	10
B Charlton	G Hoddle

7	11
M Le Tissier	D Rogers

9	8
A Shearer	J Greaves

I can hear you saying but Don Rogers never played for England. Well he should have. Besides, it's my book!

Ted Bates, the Southampton Manager, told the press "He must be the best player in the country. I rate him as the finest forward in the country today. I also believe he should be playing for England".

Bert Head, then Manager at Crystal Palace, was equally forthright. "How can you leave a player like Don out of the England side? He's fantastic".

> " He must be the best player in the country. "

Chapter 8

CALNE TOWN AND A
FAMILY AFFAIR

A big yellow Mercedes car pulled up outside our house. Tim Beasley, the Manager of Calne Town Football Club, saw Gary and I kicking a football around in the road. He beckoned me over, his craggy face peering out. Years of drinking and smoking gave his appearance that telling red hue and prominent blood vessel look. He owned and ran a supermarket but was famous locally for a football pools win a few years earlier. A new bungalow and Mercedes were testament to that. He had come into money and was happy to spend it. Good man.

"John, you are in the first team on Saturday. Radstock at home. Be at the ground for two. See you then". That was it and off he went puffing on a cigar. My county selection for Wiltshire Schools and a few games for the reserves combined with paper talk of one or two club's interest had been enough. Bournemouth wanted me to go for a trial. And Swindon Town were showing interest.

Sure enough, my selection card arrived in the post from club secretary Bert Merrett. Bert was an institution, a gentleman who seemed to have been secretary for ever. You could always hear him shouting "Come on you Lilly White's". Clubs need men like Bert. Our trainer with his magic water and sponge man Frank Henley. When he retired he passed the sponge to his son Tony.

By the nature of things my selection meant someone else would be dropped. Hold it. Playing right back and having to make way was the popular Johnny Williams, my maths teacher at John Bentley Grammar School. He was also our school football team manager. The very man who had made me Captain and helped get me in the County team – whoops!

I still remember that first match. Sammy Hale asked me if I was nervous. In truth I was not. I had confidence and knew I could play. You have to be confident to wear, as I did later that season, the first non-black boots. I got an all-white pair and wore them for a while before going back to the standard black. The first game went well. A good win, some good tackles, crosses and passes. That No.2 shirt was mine for the next few years.

The only problem was maybe too much football. I kept a record together with cuttings of our games from the Saturday night football pink.

Season 1970/71	Appearances
Calne Town	39
Wiltshire Under 19's	6
Grammar School	22
County Trials	2
Calne Youth	1
Total	**70**

The next season we had a Sunday League Team. At one stage it was Saturday morning sweeper for the school. Saturday afternoon right back for Calne Town. Sunday centre forward for C&T Harris. Crazy but in those days, it was what it was.

The Calne Town thing was special. It meant something to play for your home town team. The Wiltshire combination threw local teams together and we played teams from Swindon such as Park, Vickers, Sanford and Highworth. Wooton Basset, Radstock, Chippenham, Melksham, Devizes, Marlborough and so on across to Salisbury and Bemerton. Tim stayed as manager for another year or so. His team talks were brief. For example, if we were a goal down at half time he would say, "Right, you've got us in the shit here. Now go and get us out". He recruited a few players from Swindon including Vince Mascia who had played for Swindon Town. Tim was paying out some brown envelopes.

Finance at grass roots level is tight. The cost of pitch and ground maintenance, travel, kit, footballs, postage and secretarial function all have to be found. Insurance, payment for referees and linesmen plus hospitality to the away teams all have to be found.

Most clubs have fund raising events, match day ticket sales, raffles, perhaps a social club and bar. When Tim left, players were asked to sell so many raffle tickets each per week. I objected saying it was not right to expect players to sell tickets to raise money to pay players to come from Swindon and other towns to take the place of local boys. B******s to that. I said words to that effect at the AGM. I also wrote a letter to the committee re team selection and general ability of one manager. I still have a copy of the letter and Bert's wise response. Always the rebel! Anyway, with his payments Tim opened a can of worms. Many clubs have got in trouble and some have folded getting into financial difficulty.

By now brother Gary was in the team as a centre back. A good header of the ball and strong in defence but just a little slower than his good-looking brother. Also, at this time Dad, who was not able to just enjoy watching his sons play, wanted to be involved. He became Club Chairman. Grandfather Percy joined the committee and became responsible for money collection from supporters ground entry. He sat in the turnstile box complete with his trademark bow tie and cigar. Calne Town was now a family affair.

My role was changing A few seasons earlier, Dad and his friend and colleague Roy King reformed the C&T Harris football team. They were joint managers. Gary played sweeper. I played up front at No.9 and scored plenty. 53 goals one season. Sunday League is obviously not so strong as Saturday football, but we had a good team and quickly ran through the leagues to the top division. Great memories and laughs. I recall moving out to the wing in one game. After the Saturday night out there was no way I was going to head the ball.

I became frustrated at right back for Calne. We were not scoring so given the Sunday goals I went up front No.9. A couple of goals in the first game against Wooton Basset set the scene. That's where I stayed averaging a goal every other game. Is scoring a goal better than sex? Is that first cup of tea in the morning better than that glass of whisky at night?

I had loved scoring goals. The basic tools help. Two good feet and a nice turn of pace. At six foot I was not pushed around. As a utility player the defender in me helped with aggression and bustle up front. You remember some goals fondly. Over time I scored on pretty much all the grounds we visited. Missed a few as well. It's all part of the game. A few goals that I recall quickly would be a first minute right footed drive taken first time into the corner from outside the box against Melksham.

C & T Harris Football Team

30

A penalty to win a game at Devizes, a tap in at Park for a draw. A last-minute winner at St. Joseph's for a 1-0 win in a top of the table clash. And so on. A lob over the keeper when put through on Chippenham's ground v Devizes in a County Cup Semi Final. So what? Well, it was good at the time!

Strikers rely on good service. You need a good mix in any team. A solid goalkeeper. No nonsense defending. Skill in midfield to create openings combined with aggression to win the ball. Forwards with pace and positioning guys in the team who know how to score.

You do not need to be best mates with everyone but if you get along it helps. The odd laugh can help. On our way to Hungerford Town for a cup match I generously handed chewing gum around. It was the gum that turns blue and in turn your tongue and mouth. Only temporary boys, back to normal before kick-off. Of the players I played with, my team of that era would be, just for the record so indulge me:

	W WATSON		
2	5	6	3
I Bevan	**J Godwin**	**G Godwin**	**B Malkin**
7	10	4	11
K Moore	**A Duncan**	**P Slade**	**D Norris**
	8	9	
	M Baker	**D Powel**	

Talent is vital but so is a footballing brain. The ability to read the game. To keep the ball, to find a team mate. I'm thinking of one lad who could have made it but would just put his head down and run like a headless chicken. Another well built lad who had touch and skill but no heart and passion. Another guy who kept shooting over the bar from 40 yards and never listened when his team mates complained. They never got it.

My pet hate was to drift into a good position in the clear waiting for someone on the same wavelength to pass only to hear some mutant in the crowd shout "Get in the game Godwin".

" Get in the game Godwin "

"Next stop the Wheatsheaf!"

Calne Carnival winners

CARNIVAL TIME

Calne Carnival held a well supported six-a-side competition attracting teams from all over the County. One year we asked a local pub landlord to sponsor us. Wilf Keepence kept the Wheatsheaf, one of the best pubs in town. As kids, most Sundays Dad would walk us down to the Wheatsheaf. We would sit in the back room with a pineapple juice and a packet of Smith's salt and shake crisps. The men would have a couple of pints in the main bar. This was a proper old-fashioned pub just like 'The Bug and Spider' at the other end of town or the 'Dumb Post' at Bremhill. Wilf was a legend.

There was a back entrance through Wilf's garden. One day a regular ran into the bar shouting "Help, the Germans are coming, there's a parachute in the garden!"

Now I should point out Wilf was a slight man while his wife was a large woman.

Wilf and a few others went out to have a look. His wife's huge bloomers were blowing on the washing line. The regular was in hysterics which quickly passed when Wilf banned him for life. "You can't ban me Wilf, I've been coming in here for 20 years". "I can, and I have" said Wilf. You have insulted my wife. Get out of my pub".

Wilf agreed to sponsor us if our team represented the Wheatsheaf. All we could drink for a week if we could win.

Well we could, and we did. Wilf kept his end of the deal.

Cheers!

One we did not win was at Chippenham Carnival. For no particular reason we entered as Calne Blue Cream. Things turned ugly. We went out to a late winner from a useful player, Phil Gainey. As he scored, in frustration I made sure he on scoring was helped into the net and left hanging. After the match he stormed into our dressing room. Gary still laughs at the thought of Phil and I slinging into each other. The mistake he made was coming in barefoot. I still had my size 11 boots on. The tap dance that followed was hysterical.

While I am at it, another irritation, and I know he is a national treasure, is the commentary of John Motson for f**k's sake.

"Oh, he should have scored". Really John. Well actually mate it was less than a half chance. He did well to get to the ball and the keeper made a great save.

"His uncle once played for Bury". So what!

"His grandfather played in this fixture 52 years ago next Saturday". So what!

Not interested John. Have you not heard some of the best commentators actually do not talk all the time. I can see it was a f*****g goal. You are on TV not the radio Motty!!

❝ Oh he should have scored ❞

Football has changed and not for the better. Players swearing at the Referee and surrounding him. Get some red cards going. Holding shirts at corners. Get the penalties going. A player standing in front of the goalie sometimes not interfering with play so not offside. Really?

A player sent off for denying a goal scoring opportunity. Absolute garbage. A penalty would suffice. Why send a player off and ruin the match? I was at Stamford Bridge when a Manchester City player was sent off. 52,000 people have paid big money to see a game spoilt in the first ten minutes. A spectacle ruined by poor officialdom. You can tell a referee who has never kicked a ball himself. Football is a contact sport. Hard fair tackles are part of the game. Come down hard on the two footed in the air leg breakers. Leave most of the rest alone.

I want to pay a little tribute to 'Tiny' Spires. Tiny passed on not so long ago. He was being served tea at North Wilts Golf Club as it happens by Gary's daughter Emily. He was taken by a sudden heart attack. Tiny loved his sport, so I hope it was after a round of golf and not before. He was a loadmaster in the RAF at Lyneham in charge of what went on a plane and weight distribution. Being only 6 miles from Calne we got the odd bonus of a player or two from the RAF.

Tiny was 6'4" and all muscle. He was good in the air, a bit gangly on the ground but he played water polo for the RAF and was tough as nails. No-one messed with Tiny. Hardened tough guys and most teams had one would end up battered. Tiny ran straight through them and the ball would drop hopefully for me to pick up the loose ball and score. A pleasure to have known Tiny, the hardest man I played with. RIP Tiny.

Alongside Calne, the C&T Harris team continued nicely. When Dad and Roy King had enough of running the team Gary and Ian Bevan were joint managers before the mantle was passed to yours truly. An interesting experience.

One favourite story concerns Andy Brewer. He liked a cigarette at half time on a Sunday. One game he walked back on the pitch still having his smoke. The referee saw him, and he was sent off for smoking on the pitch! It hit the papers so much that Andy was famous for a day or two. Embassy contacted him and he was sponsored for telling everyone he always smoked Embassy!

You don't get far without a little self-promotion. One year I wrote a letter to the Chairman of Selectors basically saying I should be in the Sunday League representative team. I signed it in our then manager's name and sent if off. Come the next representative game yes, you've guessed it, straight in! Why not!

I tried wearing rugby boots for the extra ankle protection. Trust me, they do not work for football. You lose your feel and touch. I sold them after just one game to Paul Candy. He wore them for the first time away at Salisbury. He scored with his first touch running back shouting "It's the boots, they are great!" Unfortunately, this proved to be a fluke. The boots were quickly ditched.

Alan Duncan and Dereck Norris were fine players. Malcolm Baker was possibly the best all round player after me that is. Take that with a pinch of salt! I am laughing as I write and thinking of an epic cowboy 'The Man who Shot Liberty Vallance'. John Wayne turns to James Stewart and referring to Lee Marvin who was Liberty

Vallance, the bad guy in the film. Wayne said "Liberty is the toughest guy West of the Pacos. Apart from me that is". Willie Watson was a good goalkeeper in the early days apart from the home game where he dived for the ball and got kicked square in the face. Running back and looking at him was dreadful. His nose was near his ear and a cavity where his nose was. Dial 999.

My last game for Calne Town FC came when I was 26 and moving away from my home town. A career promotion meant new horizons for me and my family.

Twenty years later I received an invite to play in a charity past Calne Town versus Chippenham Town. It was great to turn out once again in the white strip. Walking down the steps from the changing room to the pitch was nostalgic. I went back and did it again in the knowledge that it was for the last time at the start of a match. A fond and pleasant see you later.

Blimey, it's fifteen years later and I've got an invitation to play again. This time it's a 65th birthday Calne v Chippenham on Chippenham's pitch organized by the family of Dereck Powel. Hold it, you've got to relax and smell the flowers at some point. This was a bridge too far. Anne and I drove up and watched the game before attending the evening party traditionally being last to bed. As for the game, very predictable. A hamstring here, a calf muscle, a bad back. Tony Lovesey, a good crosser and rugged full back from the good old days, was there. We shook hands and as he was into his seventies I said, "Glad you had the sense not to play". He opened a bag to show his old boots. "Wanted to but only brought my boots. No kit. I thought they were providing Calne and Chippenham kit. Times are not what they used to be! The game's gone backwards!"

DEVON SEEDS SOWN

One pre-season tour saw Calne Town visit Devon. Little did I know at the time, but this would have a profound influence on the future. We stayed in Teignmouth, a seaside town with a working port. We drove past the golf club that I would one day Captain. Down the hill and past the school 'Hazeldown' which my daughters would attend and later my grandsons Jensen, Billy and Harry. With panoramic views it had a good feel and we stayed two nights. First match was a visit to a strong Exmouth side. We lost that one not helped by team bonding the night before. That is code for a good night out!

I had several hours in a hot bath with a back strain. I was determined to play the next day and keep the No 9 shirt. We drew 2-2 at Tiverton Town. I got our two goals both coming from brother Gary's passes which put me through. One of my better games. I have been back there for a couple of sports dinners. It still gives me a good vibe.

Anyway, on moving as Branch Manager with Lloyds & Scottish Finance to Exeter it was a case of where to live. Teignmouth due to the football tour came to mind with its golf club, schools and easy access to Exeter, the motorway and other main roads. It seemed a good choice and 34 years later it was.

Lets Go

Chapter 9

FOOTBALL SCOUT

The telephone rang. It was Brian Hillier. Now Brian had taken over as Chairman at Calne Town from my Dad which opened the door for him to get involved in football including the pre-season game with Swindon Town. He was a good listener and shrewd. Good to spend time with. I liked him. He used Calne Town as a stepping stone and went on to be Chairman of Swindon Town. Related through his marriage to Beryl, my Mother's cousin, he enjoyed our company. He watched us play on Saturday and Sunday mornings. I last saw him back as Chairman of Calne Town at a game against Dawlish. We watched the game together, had a cup of tea half time. He asked me how I thought my style of number 9 play would suit the Calne Team today. I do not really know if that was a compliment or not.

Brian made his money at H and H Electronics. I would ring him and always get through. He knew that if there was a call from the office for awards to business and trade it was me. The first time I really got him going. He did a great job at Swindon Town taking them through the leagues to our only period in the premiership helped by his manager, the Manchester United legend Lou Macari. Lou was capable. At Sarah's wedding, Brian's daughter, he came across as a quiet orange drinking nice sort of guy but what do you know about anyone over a short period? Brian made sure we had Cup Final tickets and tickets for other games. Good man.

I had a season ticket at Torquay United. I could be sat in my lounge at 2.30 and be sat in my seat for a 3.00 kick-off. In those days you could go in pre-season and pick your seat. I had one next to the Directors box and one time when Swindon visited, Brian saw me and leant across selling me a couple of tickets to a Sports Dinner in

Swindon. He took great delight telling his co-Directors "There you are, an away game in Torquay and I'm still selling tickets".

Brian's great time at Swindon finished with a spot of bother concerning FA regulations and method of payment to players. A similar case involving Spurs was whitewashed but the book was thrown at Brian and Swindon. It was good while it lasted.

Anyway, back to the phone call. Brian was now doing a bit of scouting for Steve Bruce at Sheffield United. He said to me "What are you doing tomorrow". "Golf in the morning then I don't know". "Fine" he said. "I want you to be me. The Sheffield United scout. Torquay versus Scunthorpe. I need a report on the Scunthorpe left back". Brian knew I could help him out. I had in any case recommended a promising lad who scored a few goals, Mark Lockyer. Brian sent John Trollope down and signed him up as a trainee. I played badminton with Mark's parents, Gwen and John, a big Exeter Chiefs supporter, former player, trustee, South West selector, radio commentator and all-round good guy. Sport is in the blood is it not?

I got to the ground at Plainmoor. Had some good times here particularly when Cyril Knowles was manager. The Spurs and England left back famous for his song 'Nice one Cyril, Nice one son' did a good job over the years. Players like Tony Currie, Mark Loram, Jim McNichol and Paul Trollope, son of John, played. A young Lee Sharpe always looked a talent and was sold to Manchester United. The good days have gone for the moment. When I go to watch now I take my boots hopeful of getting a game and I am 66.

Picking up my ticket, B Hillier Sheffield United, I took my seat next to another scout from Brentford. As a one-time Torquay United season ticket holder, it felt strange. One of the Directors Dereck Hair was a friend of mine. I wanted a low profile. Dereck was to be President of Teignmouth Golf Club during my year as Captain. Great guy. A vet like Colin, his son, who at one time was vet to Newton Abbot Race Course. If an injured horse needed dispatching Colin was your man.

The first half came and went. The Scunthorpe left back looked useful but had a quiet game. The Brentford scout made copious notes on players and formations. He looked at me and said, "No notes?" I pointed to my head "It's all in here mate". Half time. Torquay on top. Hold it.

A tap on my shoulder. I turned around to see the Torquay United Chairman Mike Bateson. Mike made his money in double glazing and did a good job for Torquay. He improved the club and ground. "Can I have a word? Are you the Sheffield United scout? Come next door to the boardroom". Christ he was talking to a local Torquay supporter.

"Now, who are you watching? Who are you interested in?"

"I cannot say. It's our policy. More than my job's worth" I responded.

"Come on" he said, before saying what a Torquay United supporter did not want to hear but knew to be true. "They are all for sale you know. If the money is right."

Every player has a price. Money talks especially in the lower leagues. A cup of tea and back for the second half. I left just before the end to avoid another grilling. It had been interesting.

My report to Brian on the Scunthorpe left back "Promising, worth another look. No charge!".

Chapter 10

THE FRENCH CONNECTION

Driving down to the South of France in a battered coach with no air conditioning is not the best experience on one's travels. When going along around 60 mph the driver stands with one hand on the wheel to let his relief driver slide into the seat it becomes positively hairy. Rodeo bus journey Messrs Cowboy Coaches style. Around this time circa the 70's it was fashionable for a town to twin with another town in Europe. The Calne Town Council, in their infinite wisdom chose Charlieu way down in France. It was a similar size and word soon got out that they had a really good football stadium. A challenge went out, so we were en route. Despite the driver's antics, and the banger of a bus, we got there.

On arrival and a grand reception hosted by the Mayor of Charlieu the two football club chairmen shook hands. John Godwin Senior and Rene Parenti. Both gave a little speech. Amusing to look around. They spoke in French and did not understand English and vice versa. It did not matter. In some cases, lasting friendships were in their infancy. Years later, after visits both ways, my parents named their house Parenti.

Each player was to stay with a French family. It was pot luck. Gary and Dereck Norris together went to a bit of a run-down house complete with an Alsatian guard dog. They never felt safe. Short straw. Anne and I hit gold. We stayed with Mr and Mrs Alix. They were a little bit older than us but wonderful and kind people. What a result.

Calne Town F.C. ready to get on the bus to the South of France. Anne and I are in the front

The Alix family would later stay with us in Calne. They enjoyed sightseeing in London. Exploring Wiltshire with typical English pubs with proper beef steaks and pints of 6x direct from the local brewery in Devizes. The Alix family forged strong bonds with us as the Parenti's did with Mum and Dad. Their daughter, Annique Parenti, stayed with us for six months to learn English and got a job at C&T Harris.

Come the day of the match we were treated to a pre-match meal. It was a set up. Word went around the boys to leave the wine alone. That went for the escargots as well. Red wine and snails were not part of our pre-match routine.

For the game a good crowd turned out. The ground was of a professional standard. The teams were well matched. The clouds opened and it poured with rain. We won 1-0 with the winner coming from Alan Duncan. Splendid. The evening brought another reception and dinner. Now the gloves were off. Our boys were now drinking for England. Bring on the red wine! I must have had a good game because Mr Alix wanted everyone to know I was staying with him.

Charlieu is right in the middle of Beaujolais territory so maybe those Calne Councillors had done a little research after all.

A few years later and we were back, this time with our two young daughters in tow. The Alix family owned and lived above a chocolate shop. All manner of chocolate delights were made by Alix at the unit behind the shop. A bit like Willy Wonka's chocolate factory. The kids loved it and the produce was stunning.

The apartment above was large and spacious. Fabulous hosts. For example, I let slip that we also enjoyed Italian food so Mrs Alix arranged for an Italian chef to come around one evening to cook for us all. Unbelievable. Being a bit of a picker, eating French style suits my style. Slow, leisurely with small regular items rather than a stacked plateful. That puts me off straight away.

At one evening meal I was wearing my pride and joy. A new top of the range American baseball sweatshirt. It was the bee's knees. Jean-Charles was around 12. Isabelle, his sister, 14. He could not keep his eyes off it with its badges and numbers. After an evening of wine, fine food with both families trying to speak English, French or sign language I took the sweatshirt off. I asked if he liked it. He nodded. I gave it to him. He put it on and sat there transfixed with the widest grin ever.

Mrs Alix got her handkerchief out. Mr Alix got up with a tear in his eye. He came over and embraced me. Mes Ami, Mes Ami. He looked at me and then the old worn grey sweatshirt he had on. He had been wearing it in the heat since we arrived including trips around the Morgon and Brouilly vineyards. He had taken me shooting in a wood with his dog. Anything that moves or flies in France is fair game.

Oh my God I thought, reading his mind. Too late. Off it came. He gave it to me. I pulled it over my head or maybe it crawled over on its own. Managing not to pass out aided by a gulp of red wine we embraced again. Blood brothers and friends for life. Every Christmas until he retired a box of chocolates would arrive. The chocolate peppermints I can still taste. We are still in touch after over 40 years. Sport had again touched our lives in a good way.

We visited Annique Parenti when she had a spell in Grenoble in South East France at the foot of the Alps. Her partner being a master chef and it being my birthday he cooked us a corker of a meal. With our daughters in bed and Anne and Annique retiring the partner and I were alone. He went to the back of a top shelf in a cupboard producing a bottle and two schnapps style glasses. The idea was to take shots together straight down. This was contraband fire water. We did this for a while matching and looking at each other manfully. Any France versus England fixture should be taken seriously! We called it a draw.

Vive La France!

Jean-Charles and I after the sweat shirt swop!

Chapter 11

EUROPEAN TOUR

We would miss our Monday night games night for a few weeks. We were going on a journey. Excitement was high as we drove up to the golf club at the start of our European Tour. The CD was set to The Clash singing "Should I stay or should I go now". It was our tour song. We stopped briefly at the golf club to take in the panoramic and varied views predicting that we would not see finer on our trip.

Anne was in the front as chief navigator in pre-sat nav times being 1991. I was driving my firm's car, a light blue Vauxhall Cavalier. Fiona (aged 10) sat behind Anne and Jacqueline (aged 12) sat behind me with a comb in her hand. She had a routine of smacking me on the arm if the music was not to her liking.

Anne and I took the view that travelling was fun and educational. At lightening pace it went like this. Teignmouth 307 miles to Dover. Ferry to Ostend, Belgium. 63 miles to Brussels. La Grande Place, the Royal Palace, the E.U. Gin Palace etc. 143 miles to Luxemburg. A few deep breaths and you have seen it. With a population circa half a million how do they get a football team together? 143 miles to Saabrucken, just into Germany. Sightseeing but leisure, swimming and chilling. 125 miles to Colmar in the Alsace.

Walking in the Black Forest. Alpine type houses of different colours. Mainly wooden built. Great scenery and hillside lodge lunches. 164 miles exploring. Next Switzerland 142 to Interlaken taking in Bern and a bear pit on the way. Bern was cool, the bearpit complete with bears was not.

A week at Interlaken. Fantastic. Cable car rides, green fast flowing rivers. Scenery that in its own way challenged what we said about the view at Teignmouth. Different of course.

Up the Jungfrau in the Bernese Alps. The Jungfrau railway has been rolling along for more than 100 years making its way to Europe's highest altitude railway station at 3454 metres or 11,333 feet. You are at the top of Europe here. The views are amazing but beware the thin air. Several Chinese tourists had to sit on the floor in a state of semi collapse.

We walked around Interlaken and bought a Swiss cuckoo clock. Quite a nice one actually that now hangs in the hall. In turn our grandchildren have watched the cuckoo and little people in costume and animals pop out each half an hour. It only goes on for them. It would drive you crazy hearing the cuckoo and songs from 'The Sound of Music' 24/7.

Our luxury tent was an interesting experience for the family especially for an ex-boy scout who was press ganged into service. Our tent was on the banks of Lake Thun and we had a whale of a time. We quickly learnt the ground rules on this camp site. Gates shut at 7, no cars in or out and quiet after 10 etc. Not overly impressed with the safety i.e. security of a tent at night, we devised our own. Crisp packets on the floor, pots and pans on top of each other by the door. It gave us a laugh.

A Canadian canoe into the lake. Fiona and I were straight in for a swim around and under the canoe and yes, it was cold! Anne and Jacqueline took the view that it was too cold!

Next stop 296 miles to Auxerre in France. Apart from the Burgundy wine and Gothic cathedral it was as always good to just explore but enough of that. The highlight for sure was Saturday night at the hotel. In a square next to a church our family room was fine. The balcony looked down to the church and square. We were to find out later that the bells start early on a Sunday morning. For whom the bell tolls. Well us then!

We went to dinner early and were first in the restaurant. It was empty and quiet, almost dull. The plates, dishes and ambience showed promise and being in no rush we had a drink and relaxed. Gradually the locals turned up and it was wonderful to see well turned out, well behaved families enjoying good food and wine. A party atmosphere soon developed with music and it was just one of those special nights.

112 miles to Paris. Another run around the must-sees, mainly for the girls. Anne and I had been there before. Eiffel Tower and so on, Paris is always cool to visit. 128 miles to Le Havre. Portsmouth 143 to Teignmouth. 1771 total mileage. In and out of 5 countries on our Grand Tour. Lovely.

Racing in La Grande Place

Relaxing in Brussels

Chapter 12

USA TRUMP THAT!

What do you do when a part of your career comes to an end. A company decides to close all its branches. You have survived from 200 to 100 branches. You survive 100 to say 20 branches. You are sat running the Bristol branch of Lloyds Bowmaker Finance when the word comes. All branches to close here's a cheque and sayonara. That's Japanese for goodbye. Do you bank the money and look for a job as you probably should? No, that's too obvious. What you do is to buy a Mercedes, play golf for 6 months and take your wife and daughters to Florida. So, we did!

Donald Trump is President of the U.S.A. It seems people are fed up of the establishment not listening to them. They want change just like Brexit. Trump will build a wall on the Mexico border. He will curb Muslim immigration and finally, if you are a lady secretary in the White House, go buy yourself a chastity belt!

The jokes have started. Four passengers on a plane with 3 parachutes. It's going to crash. Passenger one, Brad Pitt, said his fans would not want him to die. He took the first parachute. Passenger two, Donald Trump, said I am going to be the smartest U.S. President ever and took parachute two. That left a 10-year-old boy and the Pope who said, "You have many years left my boy, you have the last one". "That's okay", said the young boy "There are still two parachutes". "America's smartest President took my school bag".

The good news is that President Trump likes the Brits. He just thinks the English were dumb to build that Hadrians Wall with all those great golf courses in Scotland! We had three Florida holidays when the girls were young. The Disney thing takes some beating really. We bought trainers in a store in Orlando bumping into friends from Teignmouth. As Dave Coburn said, "It's a small world". Fiona walked into Disney with her new white trainers. We bought hot dogs. She somehow squirted mustard onto her hot dog but most of it landed on her white, now yellow, trainers. She cried just like when she let go of her helium balloon in Trafalgar Square. The pigeons have a nasty way of discharging onto your head! I can vouch personally for that!

Disney is great fun for the whole family. Sure, some of the queues are long but you just need to relax and go with the flow! I lost sun glasses in the lagoon with waves that suddenly hit you. A baseball cap was lost on Thunder Mountain but so what. Epcot with different countries represented was awesome. Sea World was special.

We drove around The Keys. Key West, Key Largo. Sloppy Joe's bar was a biker's paradise. The African Queen. A 15' shark finally landed by two guys who, to secure the kill, shot the shark. Is that really fishing? Over in Miami we got stuck on Daytona Beach after I drove off the hard sand. A group pushed us back to the hard stuff with one of them summing up the scene. "You guys must be British yes?"

We learnt early on that a club sandwich America style will feed an average family for a week. We went to Cape Canaveral to check out the Kennedy Space Centre. We were lucky enough to see a space shuttle launch live but had to back off far enough for it to look like a firework going off.

Flying from Manchester on one trip we booked into a hotel for an early flight. Getting Anne and the girls comfortable it was into a taxi and get off the bus time. Old Trafford – Manchester United 2 Aston Villa 0. Mark Robbins scored two that night. Got a ticket from a tout. Full house and good start to the holiday.

Back to the U.S.A. Crocodile farms, boardwalks and hover glides through the Everglades. A week in Clearwater. Magic. The room next to us was booked for an insurance convention drinks room. Sat on our balcony and out of view a huge hand reached past me towards Anne. "Hi, I'm Buck Hayes" said our neighbour! "Do you want a drink?" I jumped up and said "Hi, I'm John, Anne, this is Buck, Buck, this is Anne". Sure, we'll have a drink. Over came a bottle of Jack Daniels.

Talking to his colleague, a rather attractive delegate from Houston, I said how much we liked America. Florida is not typical U.S.A. she said, "Come back with me to Houston and I'll show you a few muggings!"

One trip we flew into Tampa from St Louis. We had a few hours to wait in St Louis so dived into a taxi to explore. Our driver showed us the Mississippi River with its paddle steamers. We walked under the Gateway Arch. At 630 foot this monument is the World's tallest arch. Our American trips were just pure fun. So pleased we did them when the girls were young.

Anne and I have been to New York since. We did the usual sights. The Empire State Building which as a boy was known as the World's tallest building. Central Park and the Strawberry Fields Memorial to John Lennon shot when entering his nearby apartment. Ground Zero where the Twin Towers stood. Who could ever believe that tragedy. I watched TV with Fiona, my daughter, and like everyone we found it hard to comprehend. We found it difficult to believe what was unfolding. If a film had been made before this, you would have said it was too far-fetched. We all remember where we were for events like this. Kennedy's shooting, Elvis's death, Princess Diana's car accident, Flash buying a round of drinks. I am only joking! Flash pays his way like all good Wiltshire boys !.

Times Square and the central building whose billboards flashing away 24/7 have made multi millions for the owners. On the obligatory bus ride, our guide pointed out Trump Tower. Clearly a well-rehearsed routine he said, "Mr Trump is away at this time attending the birth of his next wife". Charming!

Trump's women employees were asked if they would have sex with him. 60% said "Never again".

There was of course a sporting twist on my radar, Madison Square Garden. The H.Q. The mecca of world boxing. This was a must see. Awesome. You sensed the atmosphere. To stand in the arena where so many great fights have been held. Several concert halls are in the building. Tributes interestingly to Elton John and his number of concerts there. We saw him at Powderham Castle near Teignmouth, an outside moonlit concert on the banks of the Exe. Outstanding.

We were on the last tour and in walked the tennis legend Pete Sampras. Just time to say hello. It seems that he was playing Roger Federer in an exhibition this evening. Tiger Woods, a whole host of A listers and the President were in town to see this.

Okay, it was time to get tickets. Only two obstacles. 1) A complete sell out. 2) Mrs Godwin reminded me we had Row 5 centre tickets to see "Chicago" on Broadway. Close call but we went to the theatre. Anne was not having any of it, so it was Chicago with the tennis highlights in a bar later. Marriage is all about compromise!

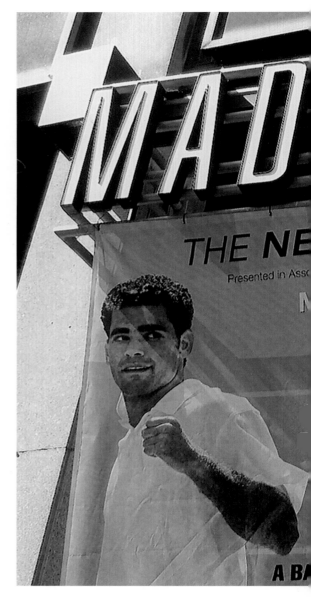

" Mr Trump is away at this time
attending the birth of his next wife "

Chapter 13

A RIOT IN ROME

We went to Rome a few years ago. What an eventful trip. It started on the M5 which ground to a complete stop a few miles from the exit to Bristol Airport. An hour later we had not moved. Our Rome trip was fast becoming unlikely. It was decision time. On the hard shoulder and off we go! Through red lights in Sandford. Anne dived into departures with the cases and tickets while I parked the car before sprinting and making the gate seconds before it closed. Such was the rush I left the car keys in the scanning tray and we had to pick them up on our return from Rome.

We met a rather nice Italian girl sat next to us on the plane. Her parents owned several chemist shops in Rome. It turned out she lived near our hotel and offered us a lift. Well, that would save a chunky taxi fare. She was met at the airport by her brother in her little VW Beetle. Before you could shout 'Gladiator' she dived into the driver's seat. I sat next to her in the front. Anne and the brother were in the back complete with all the cases on their laps. She drove like a woman possessed. 70 miles per hour, diving between cars, lorries and buses, chain smoking. The original white-knuckle ride. She screeched to a halt outside our hotel. "That was fun wasn't it?" she said. She gave us her mobile number in case we needed any help in Rome which was kind. Anne and I watched her drive away and in unison said, "Where's the nearest bar"!!

Now Rome of course is sensational. The history and sights make it quite remarkable. Complete with good walking shoes we set out to explore. We did all the usual cultural bits. The Colosseum. Now, as a fan of 'Spartacus' the film with Kirk Douglas and later 'Gladiator' with Russell Crowe, I was drawn to this immense amphitheatre with its imposing remains. You have to admire the splendour of ancient Rome. This was the centre for state functions, gladiator fights, animal hunts and circus games. You can feel the atmosphere and sense the primal fear that must have been there especially amongst the gladiators fighting to the death. The Roman Forum which served as the focal point of civil and economic life with temple remains the Basilica of Maxentius, the Curia State House, the Temple of the Vestal Virgins.

The Arch of Constantine in honour of the first emperor to recognize Christianity in the fourth century A.D. Palatine Hill, the Cradle of Rome. The Pantheon, the Spanish Steps, Trevi Fountain, every street had its own character, old and new blending nicely but mainly a sense of power and history. We had a momentous lunch at the Café Borocco in the Piazza Navona. It had been so hot looking at the sights we took a taxi to the Piazza. The lady taxi driver gave me a ten euro note which I took to be change and walked off presuming Anne had given her a twenty euro note. She had not but apparently had told me to. Net result was the taxi driver in a miff running after us much to the amusement of other tourists.

Two large beers in the café turned out to be two pint glasses. We got through them working through our salads and people watching from our outside table in the shade.

Vatican City, home to the Pope since 1377, has been an independent country since 1929. The opulence and grandeur is breathtaking. We took our time exploring St Peters Basilica with its majestic cupola at its summit. You get to walk a narrow walkway right at the top of the inside of the huge church before looking out over Rome from the outside.

The Vatican

The Vatican grottoes under ground level hold the tombs of many popes including John Paull II 2005. Standing in the square in front of the Basilica the huge dome dominates the skyline. Michelangelo began the construction around 1546, Vatican museums, the one hundred strong Swiss Guard presiding over the entrance to Vatican City, the Vatican Gardens, they're all must see's. The Borgia apartments, the Raphael Rooms and for many the tour's highlight, the Sistine Chapel. Michelangelo's masterpiece incorporating on the ceiling and walls the prophets, the sibyls, the episodes of Genesis, Christ in Judgement and so on. Remarkable colours and style.

One observation. I have never seen such a money-making machine. People queue all day every day to pay big money to get in. You want to see the museums and Sistine Chapel? Another ticket required. Allowing for costs especially upkeep. Where does all the money go? Be nice if it helped around the world. I wonder?

One evening we were enjoying our dinner sat outside a nice restaurant. It was warm and getting dark so the tables were candlelit. This was a popular spot with the locals and tourists alike on the table next to us a middle-aged couple had plenty to say. A busker played a familiar tune and our neighbour, a boisterous kind of guy, turned around and said "Hey, that tune is for you Brits". We got talking. They were Canadian. He was a munitions buyer with the Canadian Government. He asked what I did. I told him I could not talk about it.

"Hell, that's alright". I knew you were in the military right away" he announced. I asked him what he thought of Rome "Hell it's a goddam bombsight". We sure would fix it up double quick!. Place needs tidying up".

Anne and I were laughing in disbelief. If this guy had his way the Colosseum would be refurbished and the Forum knocked down and replaced with office blocks!

He was in full flow. His wife wanted fries and a McDonalds. He had taken delivery back home of a new Mercedes. 75,000 dollars and no goddam radio! He was going to kick ass on his return!

This pair were proving to be hysterical. He got up to go. They were off to Florence in the morning. "You can't go yet" I said. "I'm going to buy you a brandy".

"Sure thing" he said. "I'll drink your health any day fella".

He got up to go a little later and I said, "You can't go yet". "Why not?". "It's your round". This routine carried on for an hour with laughter. He told us all about Canada and we told them about the U.K. He wrote his address and phone numbers down which we lost. Pity in some ways because we later went to Canada. Eventually he got up and pretended to stumble into a few tables before straightening up with a grin and saying, "I'm like you, I'm as drunk as I want to be!"

So, we've enjoyed the culture. Now what sport can we home in on. Well, the Roman Games at the Colosseum finished centuries ago so we've missed that but pre-holiday planning had identified Roma v Napoli, a top Italian soccer fixture. Flying in we had a great view of the Olympic Stadium on the banks of the River Tiber. The stadium is home to the two Rome teams Roma and Lazio. Both play in Seria A. Come the day of the match we found no tickets were sold on match day. Something to do with keeping visiting fans who arrive on the day of the match

Jensen and Grampy with Totti shirts

segregated. Whoops. Undeterred we needed two tickets. If you want something or advice in a hotel, ask the concierge. Outside it's got to be a taxi driver! And so we found ourselves in a taxi explaining we want him to take us to the stadium but we have no tickets. "Ah, is a no problema". I a no a the man". A slight detour and two tickets in my pocket we are sat having a rather nice pizza outside the ground. The ticket tout has my money, the taxi driver has a tip and I have just invested in two Roma No 10 'Totti' shirts, their star player. One for grandson Jensen, one for me and a No 9 shirt for Charlie, brother Gary's youngest. Well, George, the eldest, got a Penina Golf windcheater so that seemed fair enough. Everyone's happy. Sat on the banks of the Tiber with pizza and a cold beer amongst a growing throng of Romans. Well, when in Rome ....

Going into the ground the stewards asked for ID. Well, where did that come from? We only had credit cards but talked our way in. The seats were good to the side of one goal but unfortunately exposed to the sun. It was hot but bearable with hats and sun cream. The Olympic Stadium is impressive with a 72,698 capacity. It was the centrepiece stadium for the 1960 Olympics. The running track means the pitch is a little bit further away but overall, it's a good stadium.

The game itself was lively and finished 1-1. Francesco Totti, the local hero, played. To Italians he is Gerrard, Giggs and Beckham rolled into one. The untouchable Roman Gladiator born in Rome he made his debut in 1993 aged 16. Now 38 he is still playing. 235 goals in 564 games. Like Posh and Becks over here, Totti and his wife Ilary Blasi are Italy's celebrity couple. She was a showgirl and model. When they married in 2005 the wedding was screened live on Italian TV! Totti's medals with Roma include Seria A, Italian Cup, Italian Super Cup and World Cup winner. A legend. While the game was entertaining it was overshadowed. It went something like this.

It was noticeable that the large area just twenty yards from us and being effectively in one corner of the ground was for the away fans. It's what clubs do. They give the home fans the best seats understandably. A prime example of this is at my own Swindon Town where the away supporters were given Stratton Bank at the opposite end of the ground to the Town End and behind a goal. The only uncovered part of the ground. If it rained unlucky boys and welcome to Swindon.

So, all the Roma fans were in but as kick off came and went the Napoli area remained empty. Napoli fans are notorious for trouble. Indeed, today saw them finish a five-year ban on travelling to away games so security was high but why the empty stands?

With Roma winning 1-0 all hell broke loose. We found out later that the special trains bringing the army of Napoli fans had arrived late into Rome. The fans in their anger repaid the railway by trashing the carriages as shown on TV and the papers the next day. Arriving half way through any supporter searches went out of the window as they flooded into the ground. Now, with their match and money 50% wasted and Napoli losing 1-0 the gloves were off. We had a riot being played out in front of us, literally a few yards away.

The huge security fences were being pushed and shaken but thankfully were holding. Lunatics were trying to climb them to get at the Roma supporters. Rocket flares and cannon bombs were going off in every colour and direction.

Women and children around us were crying and running away. A few Roma fans were provoking the baying Napoli fans noticeably led by a small weak looking chap who felt brave while the fence was still standing. Napoli equalized thank goodness. Having been to plenty of big soccer games in the UK and other sports around the world, this was a new experience and it just was not anything you want to see.

There was trouble brewing after the match when this rabble left the ground. We did the sensible thing and left 10 minutes early to walk along the Tiber and back into Rome. If you go to Napoli watch where you visit especially on match days!

It had been interesting at the Olympic Stadium. Fans at their worst, well actually a feral mob not deserving to be classed as fans. A crazed swollen mass feeding off their sheer noise and numbers. And here is a little footnote. When Swindon Town won the 1970 Anglo-Italian Cup, the tournament was beset by hooliganism. The final was abandoned after 79 minutes due to pitch invasions and missile barrage, tear gas was used by the Police. Swindon's opponents? You've got it – Napoli!

Chapter 14

DON'T BE SCILLY

We had a nice wedding. Anne's Dad, Phil, drove me and best man brother Gary to the Church. He pulled into his local on the way as he thought a large brandy all round was a good idea. The day went well and we drove to a hotel in Swindon. A nice meal and a bottle of wine which somehow got knocked over. Off to bed. Hold it. There was a colour TV in the bedroom. How sad. Not on your wedding night. Well let's just see what's on. Hold it. Match of the Day!! What to do! I remember watching some of the football followed by Phil Silvers as Sergeant Bilko. To this day I don't know if anything else transpired that night! No worries because we flew to Venice the next day. 'City of Lovers' for our honeymoon.

Trust the boys
to turn up with
Corner Flags

Roll on 40 years its Ruby Wedding time. Where to go? Anne had always wanted to return to the Isles of Scilly which she had visited a couple of times with the girl guides. Given the dubious sick bucket reputation of the Scillonia Ferry, flying from Exeter seemed favourite. A quick phone call to book a flight and to make sure there was a pilot and co-pilot (safety first) and we were off.

Sitting on the pilot's shoulder in our little 16-seater plane was an experience. In particular, going through cloud not being able to see anything was slightly unsettling. Landing at St Marys was a hold on to your seat job as well. A hairy drop to a small runway. On to the Tregarthens quayside hotel.

We explored the Islands and they are so quiet and peaceful. St Marys is the largest island and that is only 2.5 square miles. We drove around it on a golf buggy stopping for walks on the way. A downpour saw us take shelter in the nine-hole golf clubhouse with its view of the harbour below and it was good to check out some of its history and past members. Former Prime Minister Harold Wilson was a member with photos of him on the wall. He had a bungalow and loved to visit St Marys. He was buried here. The coastline has deserted white sandy beaches, scenic walks and trails.

Island hopping is great fun on the small boats run by friendly locals happy to share their knowledge. A highlight was the Tresco Abbey Gardens. These beautiful terraced gardens house over twenty thousand plants that thrive due to the sub-tropical weather conditions. Many of the plants would not survive in Cornwall just thirty miles away.

On Bryher we explored looking for the site where the artist would have been when painting the drawing that hangs in our family dining room. We found time to visit a couple of customers who we had helped finance ATVs and farm equipment. It was good to meet them. On to the Fraggle Rock Café and Bar for refreshments. Splendid.

We found Anne's old Seend Girl Guides camp site in Middle Town on St Martins. Really back to nature. The only pub on the island had just re-opened which was a comfort. A pint and a ploughmans went down well.

We picked up on the famous Gig Racing. For twenty-seven years the World Pilot Gig Championships have been held off the Isles of Scilly. Crews come from as far away as Holland and the U.S.A.

Most crews however come from the South West where the wooden pilot gigs are built and raced. Years ago, acting as a pilot and guiding ships through the treacherous waters off the Isles of Scilly and Cornish coast, was a well-paid job. The first pilot gig to reach the ship would get the contract and much needed money. The gig has six rowers and a coxain. Competition was fierce, and this survives to this day. A unique sporting event.

The Atlantic is unforgiving. Shipwrecks were common years ago and wrecking was rife. The aptly named HELL BAY has to suffer waves which may have been gathering momentum for 2,000 miles. The fields growing flowers for export have high hedges to keep the wind out. The Tregarthens Hotel looked after us well with great food and accommodation.

If you want a little relaxation, then try the Isles of Scilly. Don't go in the winter as I'm told it shuts!

Chapter 15

A WORLD CUP FINAL AND CANADA

Let's be totally honest. When booking most holidays, I have an eye on including a sporting event. It's who I am. Canada was no different. I was aware that the FIFA Ladies soccer final was scheduled for Vancouver, so it was no coincidence that we were to finish our holiday there. I was also aware it was a sell-out but hey, we can't be put off by little things like that.

Canada was good. The second largest country in the world. A vast country of forest trees, mountains, river valleys, wilderness, scenic contrasts and beauty. We started in Calgary. Each year in July visitors come from all over for the world-famous Calgary stampede. This combines rough, tough rodeo's, chuckwagon races, the Grandstand show, world-class agricultural activities, one of Canada's largest music festivals and heart pumping rides at North America's largest mobile midway show.

In the Indian village, step back in time with authentic plains Indian cultural practices. At the stampede held in and around Stampede Park, take your pick from bull riding, barrel racing, rodeos. Over a million people visit the ten-day event.

We enjoyed the vibrant atmosphere of Calgary. The old town combines with modern malls. I was, as a cowboy nut, taken with the cowboy stores, authentic boots, jackets and memorabilia.

We went up the Calgary Tower and were very impressed to witness Canadian Special Army Troops dropping off the top as we stood in the viewing area as high as you could be. They were taking abseiling practice. Going up in the lift I spoke to one of them. It was to be his first 'big one'. His eyes told me he was up for it but maybe it was a little higher than he expected at 626 feet tall!

On to Banff and its busy town and river walk. Up cable cars for spectacular views. Panoramic. A helicopter ride up into the Rockies at Capmore. Our taxi was late and the driver gave us a white-knuckle ride to make up time. Turned out he literally was a race driver at the weekends. The racetrack was next to the heliport. The weather was poor and rainy. I told Anne, Alan and Diane that I was out of the chopper ride. Alan explained that to keep any street cred I had to man-up regardless. Well it cleared a bit and there we were. Onwards and literally upwards in our 5-seater chopper including our young pilot who, in fairness, seemed to know what he was up to!

On to Johnston Canyon for a morning river gorge walk, cold but invigorating. Lake Louise for fine dining and top hotel on the gorgeous lake. Moraine Lake and on to the ice fields. A ride on the Athabasca Glacier aboard one of the huge specially made snow coaches. Stepping out on the glacier for a walk. Awesome.

Lake Louise

Jasper National Park, the Athabasca river

Now on to Jasper in Western Alberta. Not big but the commercial centre of Jasper National Park located in the Canadian Rockies within the Athabasca river valleys. Approaching along the sensational winding river I knew I had seen the river before. A minute or so later this was confirmed when the guide announced that 'River of No Return', a cowboy starring Robert Mitchum and Marilyn Monroe, had indeed been shot here. It's in my cowboy collection. Jasper was fine with its bars and our hotel featured a museum underground complete with a large collection of stuffed animals. Elks, bears, beavers and so on. The main railway line ran through and we were booked on the world famous 'Rocky Mountaineer' to take us over two days down to Vancouver. One of the highlights of the trip.

The Rockey Mountaineer through the Rockie Mountains, peaks, valleys, winding cascading rivers of course was a one off. On tap fine dining, drinks and service all day. Well informed guides. An overnight at Kamloops where we shared a touch of vertigo as predicted by the guide and then down to Vancouver ready to board 'The Noordam' ship en route to Glacier Bay in Alaska. Super!

We were on a seven-day return trip from Vancouver to the Margerie Glacier at Glacier Bay, Alaska. Once there, the ship stopped close under the glacier for an hour or so to let us watch first hand as huge chunks of ice crashed from the glacier into the sea. I guess that's part of the global warming effect but also it seems the glacier slowly builds up anyway and moves as pressure builds and forces a forward push towards the sea. Either way, it was spectacular. On the way up and back the ship docked to allow trips off including Juneau and onto a smaller boat for whale watching. Whales dived around us. Unbelievable. Skagway and another scenic railway trip up the White Pass and Yukon Trail. Real gold prospecting territory.

On the train, two older male Japanese tourists caught my attention. They were taking photos from every angle diving in front of anyone in their way like a pair of selfish, demented kami kazi pilots. Near the end of the trip our excellent young guide explained how any tips would be appreciated towards his college fees. Everyone tipped apart from the Japanese guys. I caught the eye of one of them as I tipped and made a gesture for him to do likewise. He stared and said in good English, "Do you think you are doing the right thing?" "Yes of course, it is the custom and education is a fine thing. It can help the world avoid ignorance and mistakes". Only good manners and a holiday spirit stopped me saying "Remember Pearl Harbour?"

The Red Onion Saloon in Ketchikan was memorable as was a tour on the amphibious duck lorry around the old town and then off the dock into the harbour to see seals and other wildlife.

Tragically, a few days ahead of us, a seaplane taking guests on a sister ship for a ride had crashed at Misty Fjords National Park killing seven people. We gave the seaplane to Misty Fjords a miss in favour of down time in 'The Red Dog Saloon'. This was epic especially the Honey Bourbon hot toddy made up of Alaskan Outlaw Whisky, honey liqueur, hot water and lemon. Like your favourite chocolate, one is never enough so we had several!

Forest fire at Whistler

Back to Vancouver for a few days' exploration and a day trip to Whistler. A huge forest fire meant poor visibility and air quality. We saw the Winter Olympic Village from the Winter Games but were glad to get out. I bought a protective air filter mask from a workman it was that bad and have the photos to prove it!

Now my mind was on the football final. On the 'Noordam' I had kept in touch with the scores. At dinner one evening I asked one of the crew to find out the Canada v England quarter final score. On the next table a couple of feet away sat two Australian men complete with their wives. A Crocodile Dundee lookalike said, "Yes and while you are at it cobber, try and get the Australian result against the f....ing Germans". His wife told him to watch his language in front of us to which he replied, "That's alright Mavis, they are Brits and hate the f....ing Germans just like we do!"

I was feeling holiday friendly so said to Crocodile, "Well the ashes start soon in England. Your boys are over for the series. Let's raise a glass to the Ashes". "Think your gonna

f….ing win then do you, fancy your chances, should have picked Kevin Pieterson!" said our charming verbally challenged Aussie stereotype. "It will be a close series" I replied. "Yeah, sorry if I was a bit aggressive, sure I will drink to the Ashes" he said. "Don't apologise" I said. "It's okay, after all you are Australian!" We all laughed and toasted the Ashes which we went on to win just for the record Crocodile.

The steward brought news of a defeat for Australia which got a "Oh f...k me" from Crocodile and a 1-0 win for England to which Crocodile said "Oh well done mate, you've knocked the f...ing hosts out so enjoy the rest of your holiday in Canada. You'll be as popular as kangaroo shit over here mate". Charming fellow.

England went out in the semi-finals and we were left with USA v Japan. As explained earlier, I had got off the tour bus and secured a ticket.

Inside the stadium complete with water on a really hot day the atmosphere was great. I had no idea women's soccer had taken off like this. The 52,000 full-house were really up for what was to be a truly entertaining match with soccer and skill of a really good standard. Most of the crowd seemed to be women, families and friends creating a carnival feeling around the ground. I hit the jackpot with my seat bearing in mind I was in the lap of the gods with my random purchase.

Around thirty rows from the pitch with a great view to the side of one of the goals. Perfect. Sat to my left a charming lady who could have been an ex-Miss USA with her two children. To my right, Stan, who had driven up from Seattle USA for the game. He was a retired University Lecturer and former soccer coach who knew the USA goal keeper. He was twenty stone plus and almost spilled over on to my seat! We got on famously.

The BC Place Stadium is home to Vancouver Whitecaps F.C. who play soccer and BC Lions who play Canadian football. It is modern and multi-purpose hosting concerts and other events.

The final was interesting on many levels. Now when teams are introduced men will cheer or clap. For this game, when the names were announced the ladies screamed. What a noise. During the game the chant was USA, USA, USA while the outnumbered Japanese responded with 'NIPPON', 'NIPPON, 'NIPPON'.

The goal I was behind saw a remarkable four USA goals in the first sixteen minutes against a Japanese defence previously solid in the tournament. Carli Lloyd scored a hat trick in the 3rd, 5th and 16th minutes. Holiday 14th and Heath 54 minutes made if 5 for USA. Ogimi 27th and an own goal on 52 minutes made it 5-2. USA World Champions.

A quick exit, taxi to the hotel and out for dinner at Don Francesco on Burrard Street. Lobster Bisque and Peppered Fillet Steak, epic, to round off a rather nice day and finish our Canadian experience.

Chapter 16

THE FAR EAST AND RACE TO DUBAI 2010

So, it's official. A team meeting with our travelling companions Diane and Alan and we are going to East Asia. The usual routine, the girls plan the itinerary and then I do my two contributions namely come up with the dosh and see what sport I can sneak into the holiday. Now let's check the calendar in the countries we will be in!

Hong Kong Rugby Sevens wrong time of the year, Singapore Grand Prix, no. Horse racing, no. Football, cricket, no. Wrong part of the world. What to do, what to do!! Hold it. Eureka. We change planes in Dubai and what happens around the time we fly?

Through the European Golf Tour season played across four continents they play most of the year. 45 tournaments in 28 countries building up to the climax, the Race to Dubai, World Tour Championship in November. Now let's check the dates, well, how nice. It ends on November 25th, Anne's birthday. Lucky girl. Let's give her a special birthday. Change the flights to include a few extra days exploring Dubai and go to the golf. Isn't life good? Well, it will be when I convince the girls!

Easier than I thought. Job done. We are going to the golf. It's played at the Jumeirah Golf Estate. Let's get tickets. Wow, the cost surprises me! They are free!!

It seems the cost of getting to Dubai and other local factors meant that the tour and course owners want to encourage people to go! The players who qualify on earnings and points achieved through the season do not need any encouragement. The prize fund is 8,000,000 dollars.

And so, it came to pass that on the way home after our East Asia adventure we touched down again in Dubai aboard our Emirates Airways plane. Instead of a few hours we were staying three days. We arrived early in the morning on day 25 of our trip.

Ian Poulter and Ernie Ells on the 18th

All on display
Ryder Cup
U.S. Open
The Open
U.S. P.G.A.
Race to Dubai

A walk along the fast-flowing Dubai salt water creek which flows through the centre and connects the trading port to the desert. A red bus city tour taking in the spice and gold souks (markets) and Dhows (boats) Jumeirah beach resort. The Burj Al Arab Hotel world famous for its design and opulence. The Burj Khalifa the tallest structure in the world at 830 metres. Book into the Arabian Courtyard Hotel and Spa. Indian meal and bed. Goodnight.

Day 26-5.00 am

What is that noise! Well it was booming out. Wailing music and chanting on speakers all over the city. Well it turns out the locals pray a lot and part of the deal there you hear it whether you want to or not! That prolonged, mournful, suffering, high-pitched wail once heard is never forgotten. The Muslims of the United Arab Emirates take Islam serious man!

So, it's off to Dubai Museum, markets again of silks, clothes and spices. Into the gold souk area and earrings and necklace purchased for Anne's birthday. A water taxi and another red bus tour.

Day 27

We are in a taxi on our way to the golf. The heat in the taxi is unbearable. Our driver is from Afghanistan. He explains he wants to send money back to his family. Unfortunately for us it's his first day driving the taxi and he does not know how the air conditioning works. After driving around in circles for a while it seems he does not know Dubai very well either. The clue was when the Burj Khalifa appeared several times. Driving past the world's largest building leaves no room for doubt.

Eventually our driver stumbled on to the correct road. The entrance loomed in front of us and we were looking forward to getting out. Our driver then proceeded to miss the turning. Being a dual carriageway, it meant a four-mile round trip to get back. He agreed to stop the meter running and understood his family were not going to get fat on his tip from this particular fare!

We enjoyed the golf. The heat remained oppressive. Drinking plenty of water, sun cream and shade were all essential. Robert Karlsson of Sweden won at 14 under par after a play-off with Ian Poulter. The players had to wear long trousers even in that heat. The Ryder Cup, British Open, USA PGA, USA Open and Race to Dubai trophies stood together on display with appropriate security. The golf was good, and we were up close and on top of play due to the layout and smaller crowds than major championships get. A lovely sporting end to a great trip. Happy Birthday Anne!

In case you were wondering what happened on the first 24 days of the trip, here is a real quick short bullet whistle-stop ride. Don't blink or it will be over!

Day 1

Heathrow and away. Airbus 7 hours Dubai. Alan sat next to a dying Indian coughing and spluttering with a blanket over his head. Swapped planes in Dubai after celebrating Alan's 60th with orange and cake. No booze to be found, Alan not impressed.

Day 2

Arrive in Singapore. Shangri La Hotel. Wonderful 5 star and girls serve drinks in the lounge on their knees at the tables. Anne and Diane said "Don't even think about it". Major drink to set the tour standard.

Day 3

Sentosa Island via the docks. 24 million containers per annum. Monorail then cable car over the bay back from Sentosa – Singapore. Freaked me out man! History of Singapore Museum, Butterfly Park, Underwater World. Trip on the Singapore Flyer (think London Eye), look down at the Grand Prix circuit. Taxi ride noting football pitch built in the harbour (not much land) and a little cameo of Alan trying to have a conversation with a toothless deaf and dumb driver. Walk down Orchard Road. Italian meal, Buona Notte.

Day 4

Walk to Singapore Botanical Gardens. Humid heat, wet shirts, ginger and orchid gardens. Taxi to Little India. Alan ignored the driver. Back to the Shangri La. Swim and foot massage by the pool. Evening at RAFFLES Hotel Long Bar. Singapore Sling drinks with swing band.

Day 5

Joined Diamond Princess ship and sail.

Day 6

At sea doing a Rod Stewart (sailing).

Day 7

At Ko Samui, Thailand. Trip ashore cancelled due to flooding, health and safety. I want my money back! Quickly forgotten in the bar. Carry on doing a Rodney to Bangkok.

Day 8

Bus to Wat Trimitr, Temple of Golden Buddha world's largest statue of Buddha made in gold weighing 5.5 tons. Royal Grand Palace grounds and buildings with the Wat Prakes emerald Buddha. River cruise Chao Phrya River, the Venice of the East, aboard a long engined 60 feet canoe boat looking at shanty dwellings on the river homes regularly flooded. Overtaken by a 20 feet plus python snake in the river with a head bigger than a football. LOCAL CHILDREN SWIMMING ON THE OTHER SIDE.

Day 9

At sea. Steward told us children are taught the only way to escape if a snake starts to coil around is to bite it as hard as you can. Man's toxins are poisonous to snakes. Well that's a useful tip then.

Day 10

Vietnam. Trip to Ho Chi Minh City (Saigon). Sea Goddess Temple, Chinatown, National History Museum and Vietnamese Water Puppets. Notre Dame Cathedral, French Colonial Post Office. Ho Chi Minh Park, Reunification Hall the former palace with tanks which breached the gate in 1975 at the end of the Vietnam War.

Day 11

Nha Trang. South Central Vietnam. A tender ashore. Freak wave crashed over several of our fellow tourists. Funny to all except those now nearly drowned and soaked! Sightseeing Ponagar Cham Tower/Temple. To enter, bare feet only. Disgusting squelchy floor last cleaned centuries ago. Cue health and safety please!

Day 12

At sea. Massage and pampering for the girls followed by major incident. I call it THE SOUTH CHINA SEA INCIDENT.

The South China Sea can be very unforgiving and rough. We were amazed at night by the fishermen whose boats came out with lights blazing to attract the fish. The boats appeared together like townships. My theory was the more lights the bigger the attraction plus safety in numbers. Several mornings we awoke in our top floor rear facing cabin feeling the swell of the ship and looking down at the angry sea. The option was easy. Stay in bed and wait for Anne to return from breakfast with rolls and coffee. Bless her.

One morning I went out on to our balcony for some air dressed only in a tee shirt and shorts. In the background I heard Anne shout that she and Diane were going shopping as she slid the balcony door across. After a few minutes feeling cold and wanting the bathroom it was time to go in. Hold it. In sliding the door across Anne had locked it. The first twenty minutes were miserable. I thought of climbing over to the Yates' cabin, but one slip would mean falling into the sea and certain Davy Jones Locker or shark sandwich time. Star jumps to keep warm helped for a minute until fatigue set in. Tired, cold, wet and still wanting the bathroom after 40 minutes I was in trouble. I was pondering frost bite which toes would be amputated. With nothing available to smash the glass door and bereft of options the door clicked as Anne opened it saying, "Alright then, we've had a good shop." I will leave my response to your imaginations darlings. Happy sailing!

> **" Alright then, we've had a good shop "**

Day 13

Hong Kong. We are met on the quay by Anne's cousin John Garrett. He works in shipping and resides in Hong Kong with Jackie, his lovely wife. John has commandeered his company's private launch so we enjoy a tour of Hong Kong harbour and beyond just the four of us tourists, John complete with launch captain and a maid to keep the wine flowing. Thank you, John. We see the sights including tower blocks complete with huge holes built into them to allow dragons free passage from their mountain homes to the sea! Feng Shui is important in Hong Kong connecting to the energy of the earth. Proper positioning and flow paths superstitions persist even today.

On to Victoria Peak, Stanley Market. Evening harbour light and laser show as we sail out of Hong Kong.

Day 14/15

At sea.

Day 16

Shanghai – China. Peoples Square cultural centre, children feeding birds in the park, drive along the Bund, Jin Mayo Tower with a speed lift 88 storeys to the top and views inside to the lobby below.

Day 17

Another Rodney.

Day 18

Nagasaki Japan. Walk around the town noting the shipyards. Visit to the Peace Park with gift statues from other nations. The remarkable PEACE STATUE. The right hand points up symbolizing the atomic bomb. The left hand holds out for peace. The eyes are shut in memory. The atomic bomb museum highlighting the cruelty of war. No mention of Pearl Harbour. We stood on ground zero where the bomb dropped. A plaque notes the radiation can last up to 75 years. 1945 to 2010 equals 65 years. Hold it! No wonder my feet glow in the dark!

Nagasaki and Hiroshima both had an atomic bomb dropped on them within 3 days in August 1945. This drastic action by the USA effectively ended the Second World War. Nagasaki is rebuilt now and looking down on it from the Glover Gardens you can only imagine the horror when the bomb dropped. The original target the City of Kokura had thick cloud cover, so Nagasaki became the unlucky secondary target. The plutonium bomb 'FAT MAN' was dropped. Numbers varied but by the time injuries developed into fatalities the Nagasaki Prefectural Office put the deaths at 87,000.

Day 19

South Korea – Busan Town Centre, fish market.

Day 20

At Sea

Day 21

Beijing, China for four days. From the ship we were met by our private guide plus minibus and driver. 4-hour journey through fogged up motorway, 20 lorry jack knife accident, drivers fighting police, nearly hit a bollard. Eventually sanctuary of Beijing Hotel. Evening meal in typical local restaurant.

Day 22

Major tour with our guide. Tiananmen Square site of 1949 New China founded by Chairman Mao. Parliament Building i.e. Great Hall of the People. Mao's Mausoleum. Peoples Platform building, monument to Peoples heroes. The Square will hold a million people.

Forbidden City – Gate of Heavenly Peace – upright and Meridian Gates, Hall of Supreme Harmony – Palace of Heavenly Purity – Imperial Garden. Above all, a sense of history!

On to the Summer Palace, gardens and lake. The Imperial Residence April to October. The Temple of Heaven over twice the size at 217 hectares as the Forbidden City. Many temples to pray for good harvest. A tea shop to try different varieties. Would have preferred a distillery.

Our Guide for three days. Her English was better than our Chinese!

Day 23

Jade factory and Buddha purchase. The Valley of the Sacred Way – Ming Tombs. The Great Wall of China and a walk on the Badaling Section. Very cold and while respecting the history. Guess what, it's a wall folks. Each section much the same. Anne, Diane and Alan kept walking. I retired early to the café for coffee and a brandy with our rather charming guide for an insight into her family's history and culture.

Back to Beijing. Planning our evening I told the guide I could use a good duck. Something was lost in translation as she explained that was not covered in the itinerary costs. Not only that but she had a boyfriend. However, she had a cousin who as … Hold it. I explained I wanted a Peking Duck for which the area was famous. After a little bit of giggling she booked a table at a nice restaurant. We took a rickshaw ride and visited a typical Chinese house in Old Beijing Hutong. Bit grim to be honest but there you go. The meal was great. One of the best ducks I've had!

Day 24

Off to the silk market. Bartering, row upon row of clothes. You run the gauntlet of Chinese trying to get you to buy. We bought a few items adjusted perfectly to your measurements in the basement below. I bought some tight black and brown Mick Jagger dancing trousers. Must wear them sometime! Bags packed, we headed to the airport en route to Dubai and the golf.

It's only a wall!
Great Wall of China style

Chapter 17

CRICKET

Cricket on the village green. Ball on Willow. Tea between innings with cheese and cucumber sandwiches. Quintessentially English. The joy of a hot summer's day with the sun out to stay making a good day's cricket possible. The anguish of rain setting in meaning at best a delay, at worst no play possible. The delight of taking a good catch, the dismay as the ball hits your wicket. The frustration of a dodgy leg before wicket appeal going against you maybe by an opponent provided umpire. The banter and a beer in the local after play.

One of my early memories was watching our local C&T Harris cricket team. They had a superb private ground the pitch manicured, the wicket rolled by its own groundsman. Roy King, a fine opening bat looked well set for some runs when there was a loud "Hows That" appeal for lbw. Our home umpire gave him out, raising his finger to signal the decision. Roy's head went down and as he walked off he looked at Reg and was heard to say "You can't give me out Reggie, you're my brother" which of course he was. My uncle Phil was a class act bowler. He was medium pace but accurate. He played for Calne for over twenty years. The cricket and soccer seasons overlapped which meant you had to choose your sport for part of the year.

John Davis, my friend, was the most talented batsman around. He scored bucket loads of runs batting No. 3 for Calne and should have been snapped up by Somerset. He was a Graham Gooch in the making until I helped finish his career.

My wife Anne and I were an item in our early twenties. Her best friend Joy was home from Cardiff University, so we invited her out one evening. She wanted to come but did not want to be the gooseberry on her own. Did I know anyone to make up a four? Enter John Davis. We have just been to their Ruby Wedding Anniversary! A wonderful couple, lifelong friends who have three great kids. My godson Mark, Lucy and Lorna.

Anyway, John and Joy got together which was good on the domestic front but which 'stumped' his cricket. Shall we just say that Joy 'limited his overs'.

My own preference was soccer. As a result, my cricket never really got going. I recall at school frustrating bowlers by just sticking around and slowing things down. Okay, we may not win but guess what, neither will you sunshine. Playing for Calne I went into bat and fondly remember Uncle Phil who by now was umpiring a bit standing at my end of the wicket. I hit two fours off the first two balls and he said, "Didn't know you could bat like that John, fill your boots". The third ball landed flush on one of those boots before taking the stumps out. "Missed opportunity, you're out" said Uncle Phil. Really? I don't need an umpire to tell me that. The clue came when the ball smashed into the wickets!

John Davis would have scored plenty that day. He had a good eye, patience and timing. His driving of a cricket ball was rather better than his driving of a car. On that first date for John and Joy the four of us went to a night club in Bristol. John borrowed his mother's car. We had a good night, but it decided to snow and the roads were icy and treacherous. John did well to get us home in one piece as the car slid all over the place. Joy must have been impressed because they swapped phone numbers and were up and running. Anne and Joy were always close. Anne even sent Joy to my stag evening at Calne Town Football Club's end of season disco just to keep an eye on me. Charming.

Most amateur teams have a couple of star players who do the lion's share of the batting and bowling. Probably one will be Captain. Others contribute and maybe a couple making the eleven up. Happy to be involved, take the air and field down at third man out of harm's way.

Back in the day kit was not so good. Pads were not so well padded or strong. No helmets were worn. The old box protectors at amateur clubs should have carried a health warning. Fair enough you wanted to guard your valuables as a cricket ball can do serious damage but really some of those old box's carried more health risks than a trip to a brothel! Crushed or infected testicles is one hell of a thing to factor into a friendly game of cricket.

In recent years and armed with a little money and wisdom when asked to play for the Trinity Tennis team in a game of cricket against a touring Cardiff Cricket Team I purchased my own state of the art box coming these days nicely fitted into a pair of cricket briefs. Success, I've made it! It's all been worthwhile.

One of the team who I will call 'Charlie' got wind of my deluxe box. "Godders" he said "I am in next, can I borrow your box? The one in the kit bag looks disgusting and I don't want one from whoever's out next when it's been around their sweaty knackers".

"No Charlie, you may not. Buy your own you tight git"

"Oh come on man, help a mate out"

"No Charlie, besides with your reputation I have no idea where your balls have been. I cannot risk infection my old son. You're on your own"

"Well b******s to you Godders" said Charlie with feeling.

"My point exactly Charlie and yours could be about to get crushed. Good luck".

I took a couple of tasty catches at slip in the match which ended in a highly creditable draw and I was pleased that my eldest grandson Jensen was there to witness that his Grampy can still move. In fairness we play a bit of tennis. He won the Under 10 trophy at our local club. We also play a bit of football. I've got him standing on the near post for corners and he understands when playing for his local team it's a good ploy. The near post should be the first spot the football passes from a corner so plenty of opportunity to score.

He has a good sense of humour. At the Golf Club recently he stood in the entrance complete with his latest haircut complete with gel and asked if it was okay for him to enter the Club House.

"Of course, why not?" I said. "Well it's just that the sign over the door says NO SPIKES ALLOWED IN THE CLUB HOUSE". Jensen along with Billy and Harry, our other grandsons, are great characters who I am sure will all do well.

I had the same sports bag for over twenty years. It was like a doctor's bag really. I kept everything in there. Bandages, liniment, spare studs, toiletries, towel and even a toilet roll as some of the grounds could be basic. If ever asked to help a team mate out it would start the old one sheet only routine which would get the boys laughing.

The bag was worthless but personal to me. After playing golf at Long Ashton, Bristol, someone kindly smashed my driver's door window and stole it. Thank you for that and also for the drive down the motorway to Teignmouth. Ninety miles on a cold night with no window.

Watching local cricket and also Somerset at Taunton gives me pleasure. The ground at Taunton is compact but welcoming. The Botham Richards and Garner era has long gone of course but Marcus Trescothic can still play a bit.

We liked to sit in a corner outside the Stragglers Bar. It was more of a wooden pavilion really but the beer was good and it attracted a few characters. We were never short of a laugh. My favourite was the day a portly middle-aged chap arrived with two ladies.

He quite loudly said "Hello Harry, this is my wife Helen and this is Bridget the woman I should have married".

❝Well it's just that the sign over the door says NO SPIKES ALLOWED IN THE CLUB HOUSE❞

Chapter 18

Antigua

Early morning at Heathrow. We are in the duty-free area with our good friends and regular travelling companions Alan and Diane Yates. The girls get on well while 'Yatesey' and I are sporting nuts and compadres. At home and on some holidays we are joined by Nick and Debbie Hunt. Together Yatesey, Nick and Godders form the 3 Amigo's. Together we have been at it most weeks on the golf course at Teignmouth for over 20 years.

Anne and Diane were drawn to the perfume area while Alan and I headed to a whisky tasting table complete with a good selection of malts. The assistant had moved off for a break or to do something or other. Bit of a dilemma then. A bit early at 7.30 but we had a long trip ahead to Antigua so a drink might be in order. Self-service then and only fair to take each malt in turn! The girls and the assistant caught up with us just in time to point us in the direction of a full English breakfast before too much harm was done. We were nicely relaxed for the journey!

Antigua was fun. The usual sun, sea and sand. Nelson's Dockyard and Shirly Heights. Evenings with steel bands and limbo dancing. Nubile dancers limboing under a height of maybe two feet with the rod on fire. A whole new spin on a burning bush! Grilled chicken, fish in spices, onion and vegetable bhaji, beer, wine and local rum. A carnival atmosphere every evening.

The highlight for me a catamaran around the island. The wild rough and invigorating thrill of the Atlantic giving way to the calm of the Caribbean. The blue clear contrast against the grey. Feeling alive sat at the front point of the vessel holding on tightly pulling into an island beach for lunch and a swim. Snorkeling near a reef.

Time for a sporting twist now as always. With the girls headed for the shops and a market, Alan and I summoned a taxi. Antigua to me conjures up thoughts of cricket and Viv Richards. Let's pop into St. Johns.

Sir Isaac Vivian Alexander Richards, nicknamed the master blaster, is regarded as one of the greatest batsmen of all time. In test matches for the West Indies he scored 8540 runs in 121 test matches averaging 50 including 24 centuries. He also captained the 'Windies' 50 times. He also scored circa 7,000 runs in the one-day format and more than 36,000 in first class cricket. He played for Somerset 1974-86 and you go through the VIV RICHARDS GATES now at Somerset's ground in Taunton where the Botham Richards and Garner days are still lauded. When Garner and Richards were not retained in 1986 Botham left Somerset in protest. Loyalty to his friends but from Somerset's point of view the pair were away a lot on international duty and Somerset had finished bottom of the league. A pity all round. A poor ending to what had been overall a good period in the club's history. Let's hope time has healed the wounds.

Instructions to the driver were clear. Where does Viv live? And, we want to visit the test ground please. No sooner said than done. Mr Taxi man drove us firstly to an old area near the prison and the house the great Viv grew up in. Humble beginnings indeed. But then so many of the people of the Caribbean lived particularly historically in poverty. Money and work were often in short supply. Colonial rule, plantations and slavery were a sure thing for hardship and exploitation.

Those days thankfully have gone but only after years of struggle. I have studied the history of the Caribbean and will not expand on this here but thoroughly recommend 'A History of Antigua The Unsuspected Isle' by Bryan Dyde and Grantly Adams and 'The Social Revolution' by FA Hoyos which gives a good insight from a Barbados perspective.

The driver next drove us to Viv's house and by Caribbean standards a nice property. More modest in the UK. The giveaway was the front gate. An iron gate made to look like 3 cricket stumps to form a wicket with the initials VR above. Nice touch. You knew who you would find through the keyhole here.

On now to the Antigua Recreation Ground the National Stadium. The Antigua and Barbuda Cricket Association is a member of the Leeward Islands Cricket Association which itself links to the West Indies Cricket Board. Trust me when I tell you that in the Caribbean they take cricket seriously! Every island has its cricket heroes and Antigua can boast Messrs. Richards, Andy Roberts, Richie Richardson and Curtly Ambrose just to name four.

The ground was shut. I approached a groundsman who confirmed the ground was shut off limits and entry impossible. A couple of bank notes later and hey presto out came a bunch of keys. The grounds were open. A little pitch inspection only revealed that a local dog had been into bat before us having crept into the ground and left it's calling card in the silly mid-on area. They would not put up with that at Lords.

The pavillion and changing rooms were beyond basic but our groundsman now tour guide told us that for tests or big matches chairs and physio tables would appear. We looked at the honours boards and took a few photo's, savoured the atmosphere and then it was back to the taxi where our driver was waiting contentedly asleep. They are good at relaxation in the Caribbean. Take it easy man, relax, be cool!

On another trip Anne and I did a Queen Mary Caribbean cruise out of New York. We island hopped taking in Barbados, St Lucia, St Kitts, Tortola and St Martin. Aside from the sea and sun you could not help but to notice the number of cricket matches being played, they love it.

Just a quick one on the Queen Mary. Top class in every way. We were invited to take dinner on the table of the Chief Engineer. He insisted that all the wine was courtesy of Tom Cunnard which was a bonus. But what made me laugh was that on leaning down to pick up a napkin I noticed a torch strapped under the table by the Chief Engineer. On asking him about it he was straight to the point "If we lose power and it goes dark, as Chief Engineer I'm going to look a right plonker if I can't see to get to the engine room!" He made a good point!

Queen Mary 2 en route to the Caribbean

Chapter 19

WE WERE THERE – BARBADOS

So, it's the day before the match. Practice day. I have walked out to inspect the wicket. It looks hard and dry. Not surprising given the location. Only two people are on the pitch. One played a few games of cricket for Calne. A batsman who could hang around and tickle or nudge out a few singles mainly and, in all modesty, a good slip catcher. The other chap had also played a bit in all fairness. Leicestershire, Hampshire, England. 8231 test runs for England in 117 matches, 32 as Captain. It's the one and only David Gower and a proper gentleman. We had a little chat and what a nice man. You don't Captain England without a bit of steel and determination not to mention talent and David Gower in my eyes is an all time great. This was 1994 and we were in Bridgetown Barbados for the fourth test West Indies v England. It was pre-selfie photographs, but I wanted a photo for my office wall. Quicker than you could say "How's that!" David summoned a sky cameraman out who took the photo. We were joined by Pete my friend and travelling companion who sprinted out to join us. Not one to miss out our Pete!

Godwin, Gower and Robinson

West Indies team warming up

I saw the West Indies team warming up so decided to join them and Pete took some great photos.

England in the West Indies had been on my bucket list for some time. This trip started a few months before. It was a get off the bus moment! I asked Pete if he was in or out as I was going down to the travel agent to book. Blow me down with a feather, he said "in"! But he needed time to break it to Novella, his wife, also our close friend and good sport.

We went together to the doctor's surgery for our injections. I went first and had mine on the area you sit on before putting on a limp and agonized face for Peter. "What was it like?" he asked. "Moby Dick time Peter, harpoons!!" "You b*****d" he whispered as he walked in.

We arrived at Heathrow 3-0 down in the 5 Test series. Was it worth going? We had not won in Barbados for over 50 years. Well, we had paid our money and got our passes to travel from our wives. Let's go!

The flight over was interesting. On one side of me sat a well spoken chap complete with blazer and MCC tie. He was disgusted at being 3-0 down in the series "It's just not cricket old chap" he said. "I think you will find that's exactly what it is but we are not playing very well" I replied.

He blamed a poor attitude and lack of discipline but especially he blamed the selectors for not picking more of his Middlesex team who were good eggs.

In front of us sat a little boy aged around seven with his parents. A little turbulence or whatever and he was quite ill before his parents could find a sick bag. They called for help from a stewardess.

Our sympathetic MCC man turned to me and came out with "Oh my god. How would you like living next to people like that? Being sick right in the middle of our flight to the cricket!" I explained that while unfortunate my sympathies were with the boy!!

In Bridgetown we made it to our open plan apartment in Sandy Lane next to the famous Sandy Lane Hotel. It was basic but spacious. Our balcony was ten feet to the beach and around thirty feet of sand into the sunny Caribbean Sea. Heaven.

First job was to move the beds which were together to opposite ends of the room. That's better then! Over the next few days we took in the rays carefully, man it's hot out there. We hired an open-sided mini moke and explored the island. Four tips

1.	Do not leave anything in them. Our towels disappeared.	
2.	Do not follow a bus if you get lost. We did and ended up driving through several fields before everyone got out for a picnic.	
3.	Do cover your arms and legs from the sun unless you want to end up a shade of lobster.	
4.	Do not let Pete drive when he realises Happy Hour is approaching back at our apartment block and we are 6 miles away. Whiplash and white-knuckle ride!	

We went down in a submarine, got very familiar with Banks Beer, the island's own nectar. We enjoyed a number of bars where the cigarettes produced a smell and reaction from the locals not familiar to us. Relax man! Jungle book snake eyes. Trust in me!

Our location was great. I have been back several times, but our apartment block is long gone and re-developed in what is a prime location. Security is also stricter at the Sandy Lane Hotel as visited by Michael Winner, the film director and writer. I miss his restaurant reviews and wit. Pete and I were able to walk in and check it out.

Tim Rice was there with a nice-looking lady. Nothing unusual in that then. I had met him before at a charity function in Henley on Thames. Fun character, charming, witty and a huge cricket fan. In the bar I ordered two large whiskies which, being Pete's round, seemed a good shout. Expensive man! "Shall we have another?" said Peter. "At these prices we're off mate" I replied. "B*****d" said Pete.

I booked an early morning round of golf at the Sandy Lane Golf Club. Pete, a non-golfer, left me to it. A nice round and first sighting of some of the monkeys that can be seen on the island. One career best iron from around 150 yards to a few inches from the pin and no-one to see it. Or so I thought. "Good shot man" and a gentle clap from a green keeper resting behind a tree. Thank you.

After the round and reading the notice board outside the club house, I noticed a charity event coming up before the test. Teams of four. I was drawn towards a slot for Gary Sobers team and had no hesitation in writing my name down. John Godwin (Godders) Teignmouth Golf Club. Before the pencil was back in my pocket I was joined by a chap I took to be the Secretary. "Excuse me sir, but what are you doing?" "I've put my name down with Gary Sobers". "No sir Mr Sobers team is already full." "Okay then, I will withdraw from the team". "You cannot withdraw sir because you were not selected in the first case!" "B******ks, I said, we are just playing with words." "Let's just say I am no longer available!!" We shook hands. Incidentally, the Gary Sobers team did not win. Poor team selection!

The thing was that my daughters Jacqueline and Fiona were the same age as Pete's daughters Lyndsey and Karen. They played and grew up together. We all got on and had done for years. I had arranged before we left for flowers to be delivered to Anne and my two girls. A nice bouquet each to show I was thinking of them. The families were lunching together when Pete decided to ring home to keep in touch and also to get Lyndsey's piano exam results. He came back looking rather crest-fallen. "I've rung home just to get a b*******ing*", he said. "You sent flowers you b*****d! You set me up!".

Pete suffered for years for his solo holiday to the Caribbean. Only a trip to Florida both families together eased his torment!

We ate out one night in the French quarter at a good restaurant. Jimmy Adams who was playing for the West Indies was on the next table with some of the boys. It all added to our enjoyment and feeling part of it. I tried to get Pete to the Harbour Lights night club. Pete preferred a meal and a few drinks. Twenty-five years later, do you think we should have gone Pete?

The apartment's Happy Hour was popular, and people mixed well. After a few days we were talking to a group of Londoners including a Barbara Windsor lookalike. We mentioned our wives and she cried out "Oh my good God, thank heavens for that. We had you two down as the Odd Couple!"

At the Kensington Oval for the test it was a full house. The Sky TV boys were in place including David Gower who has developed into a great commentator and link man. Our very own Richie Benaud. Praise indeed. One of my favourite Benaudism's came when the camera zoomed in on a well-dressed chap fast asleep. "Ah", said Richie, "Another hard day at the office".

The test was a revelation. We sat in the Mitchie Hewitt stand which thankfully afforded some shade. I felt for some of the tourists sat in the sun. It must have been unbearable. The seating in the Mitchie Hewitt stand consisted of concrete slabs. Now I at the time had a lower back concern originating from a Calne Town v Devizes Town football match. A ball bounced on a divot sharply sideways so instead of kicking the football I kicked air. Anyway, I made for the only row of wooden seats. It looked full but after moving a picnic hamper to the annoyance of a local, I was in. The only white face in the row and the only English supporter to boot. The thing about the Bajeans, the Barbados people, is their warmth and friendly spirit. After an hour or so we were swopping rum for whisky and a sandwich for a piece of spicy chicken.

Curtley Ambrose and his reaction when I told him England would win the test!

One trader would walk through the crowd laden with a piled tray of assorted bhaji shouting "last two", "last two". Guess what. A truly sensational test over five days. It had everything. We hit a jackpot as England played out of their skins for a famous win!

England were put in to bat. No visiting team had won a test match since the 1930's at the Kensington Oval. Our openers got us off to a remarkable start despite the efforts of Messrs Walsh, Ambrose and Benjamin. 85 for Captain Atherton. 118 for Alec Stewart. Not a lot after that apart from Graham Hick 34 and Jack Russell 38. The last five wickets went down for less than 50. 355 in total. Not too bad.

In their first innings the Windies made a poor for them 304. Chanderpaul 77, Ambrose 44, K.Benjamin 43. Brian Lara, the best batsman in the World at that time, out for just 26. Lovely. Phil Tufnell bowled well. 32 overs for just 76 runs but the hero was Angus Fraser.

A famous victory

A superb return of 8 wickets for 75. Brilliant. In one spell 4 wickets at the expense of one run from 17 balls. Work that out. We loved it.

In the second innings we lost early wickets, but Alec Stewart compiled a historic 143, the first Englishman to score twin hundreds against the West Indies. History was being made. Pete and I were having a ball loving and savouring the action, the atmosphere, the occasion. 59 for Hick, 84 for Graham Thorpe and 50 extras. Atherton declared on 394-7, a lead of 455. At close of play on day four the Windies were 47-2.

Day 5 came and our drive to the Oval was one of optimism. The carnival atmosphere amongst the locals had subsided. The island was in shock. Surely their heroes would battle back.

With Brian Lara at the wicket anything was possible. He played and looked in form as he passed 50. On 64 he hit a ball high towards us. Christ, right in the sun and, oh no, it's Tufnell underneath it. He can't catch, can he? Well, he can, and he did. Lara caught, Tufnell bowled, Caddick 64. We were going to win. Andy Caddick took 5 wickets for 63. Tufnell again did well in the heat. 36 overs and 3 wickets. Curtley Ambrose was later fined £1.000 for smashing his wickets with his bat and Tuffers gained notoriety by not declaring 4 for the Windies when he was fielding as the ball clearly hit the boundary wall. Naughty boy. But none of that mattered. He said he was not sure!

We celebrated on the field afterwards like we had won the lottery. Well that's only money. This was a little sporting miracle and we had been part of it.

Get off the Bus!

The Wisden Trophy, 4th Test

West Indies v England
England won by 208 runs
Test no.1258, 1993/94 season
Played at Kensington Oval, Bridgetown, Barbados
8, 9, 10, 11, 12, 13 April 1994 (5 day match)

England 1st innings		R	M	b	4s	6s	SR
MA Atherton*	c Lara to KCG Benjamin	85	222	165	14	0	51.51
AJ Stewart	b WKM Benjamin	118	347	221	16	0	53.39
MR Ramprakash	c +Murray b WKM Benjamin	20	63	52	3	0	38.46
RA Smith	c +Murray b WKM Benjamin	10	24	17	2	0	58.82
GA Hick	c +Murray b Ambrose	34	92	58	7	0	58.62
GP Thorpe	c sub b KCG Benjamin	7	34	21	0	0	33.33
RC Russell+	c Chanderpaul b Ambrose	38	88	56	5	0	67.85
CC Lewis	c +Murray b Ambrose	0	2	2	0	0	0.00
AR Caddick	b Ambrose	8	33	24	1	0	33.33
ARC Fraser	c Chanderpaul b Walsh	3	26	15	0	0	20.00
PCR Tufnell	not out	0	2	0	0	0	
Extras	(lb 8, nb 24)	32					
Total	(all out; 100.2 overs)	**355**		(3.53 runs per over)			

Full of wickets 1-171 (Atherton), 2-223 (Ramprakash), 3-242 (Smith), 4-265 (Stewart), 5-290 (Thorpe), 6-307 (Hick), 7-307 (Lewis), 8-327 (Caddick), 9-351 (Fraser), 10-355 (Russell)

Bowling	O	M	R	W	Econ
CEL Ambrose	24.2	5	86	4	3.53
CA Walsh	24	3	88	1	3.66
WKM Benjamin	22	4	76	3	3.45
KCG Benjamin	20	5	74	2	3.70
S Chanderpaul	10	4	23	0	2.30

West Indies 1st Innings		R	M	b	4s	6s	SR
DL Haynes	c Atherton b FRaser	35	62	51	5	0	68.62
RB Richardson*	c Atherton b Fraser	20	67	30	3	0	66.66
BC Lara	c sub b Lewis	26	60	45	5	0	57.77
KLT Arthurton	c +Russell b Fraser	0	3	3	0	0	0.00
JC Adams	c Thorpe b Fraser	26	144	68	3	0	38.23
S Chanderpaul	c Ramprakash b Tufnell	77	305	231	10	0	33.33
JR Murray+	c Thorpe b Fraser	0	2	2	0	0	0.00
WKM Benjamin	c Hick b Fraser	8	15	13	1	0	61.53
CEL Ambrose	c Hick b Fraser	44	122	74	5	0	59.45
KCG Benjamin	not out	43	117	82	4	1	52,43
CA Walsh	c Tufnell b Fraser	13	27	17	2	0	76.47
Extras	(lb 1, nb11)	12					
Total	(all out, 101.5 overs)	**304**		(2.98 runs per over)			

Fall of wickets 0-51* (Haynes, retired not out), 1-55 (Richardson), 2-55 (Arthurton), 3-95 (Lara), 4-126 (Adams), 5-126 (Haynes), 6-126 (Murray), 7-134 (WKM Benjamin), 8-205 (Ambrose), 9-263 (Chanderpaul), 10-304 (Walsh)

Bowling	O	M	R	W	Econ
ARC Fraser	28.5	7	75	8	2.60
AR Caddick	24	2	92	0	3.83
CC Lewis	17	2	60	1	3.52
PCR Tufnell	32	12	76	1	2.37

England 2nd innings		R	M	B	4s	6s	SR
MA Atherton*	c Lara b Walsh	15	56	43	2	0	34.88
AJ Stewart	b Walsh	143	475	319	19	0	44.82
MR Ramprakash	c Chanderpaul b Walsh	3	21	12	0	0	25.00
RA Smith	lbw b KCG Benjamin	13	45	41	1	1	31.70
GA Hick	c Lara b Walsh	59	184	126	8	0	46.82
GP Thorpe	c Arthurton b Walsh	84	187	129	9	0	65.11
RC Russell+	not out	17	32	17	1	0	100.00
CC Lewis	c Walsh b Adams	10	8	7	1	1	142.85
Extras	(b8, lb 6, nb 36)	50					
Total	(7 wickets dec; 108.5 overs)	394		(3.62 runs per over)			

Did not bat AR Caddick, ARC Fraser, PCR Tufnell

Fall of wickets 1-33 (Atherton), 2-43 (Ramprakash), 3-79 (Smith), 4-194 (Hick), 5-344 (Stewart), 6-344 (Stewart), 6-382 (thorpe), 7-394 (Lewis)

Bowling	O	M	R	W	Econ
CEL Ambrose	22	4	75	0	3.40
CA Walsh	28	5	94	5	3.35
WKM Benjamin	22	3	58	0	2.63
KCG Benjamin	20	1	92	1	4.60
S Chanderpaul	10	3	30	0	3.00
JC Adam	6.5	0	31	1	4.53

West Indies 2nd innings	(target: 446 runs)	R	M	B	4s	6s	SR
RB Richardson*	c Ramprakash b Caddick	33	123	94	5	0	35-10
JC Adams	c +Russell b Caddick	12	82	49	1	0	24.48
BC Lara	c Tufnell b Caddick	64	118	89	12	0	71.91
KCG Benjamin	c Hick b Caddick	0	5	5	0	0	0.00
KLt ARthurton	b Tufnell	52	155	116	9	1	44.82
S Chanderpaul	c sub (N Hussain) b Hick	5	43	29	0	0	17.24
JR Murray+	c Thorpe b Caddick	5	31	21	1	0	23.80
DL Haynes	c Thorpe b Tufnell	15	57	42	2	0	35.71
WKM Benjamin	c Stewart b Tufnell	3	8	8	0	0	37.50
CEL Ambrose	b Lewis	12	43	30	2	0	40.00
CA Walsh	not out	18	11	18	0	3	100.00
Extras	(b1, lb 7, nb 10)	18					
Total	(all out; 82.2 overs)	237		(2.87 per over)			

Fall of wickets 0-32* (Richardson, retired not out), 1-43 (Adams), 2-43 (KCG Benjamin), 3-128 (Lara), 4-150 (Chanderpaul), 5-164 (Arthurton), 6-179 (Murray), 7-195 (Richardson), 8-199 (WKM Benjamin), 9-216 (Haynes), 10-237 (Ambrose)

Bowling	O	M	R	W	Econ
ARC Fraser	17	7	40	0	2.35
AR Caddick	17	3	63	5	3.70
PCR Tufnell	36	12	100	3	2.77
CC Lewis	8.2	1	23	1	2.76
GA Hick	4	2	3	1	0.75

MATCH DETAILS

Toss - West Indies, who chose to field
Series - West Indies led the 5-match series 3-1

Player of the match - AJ Stewart (England)

Umpires - **LH Barker** and **DB Hair (Ausralia)**
Match referee - **JR Reid (New Zealand)**

CLOSE OF PLAY

Fri, 8 Apr-	day 1 -	England 1st innings 299/5 (GA Hick 26*, RC Russell 3*)
Sat, 9 Apr -	day 2 -	West Indies 1st innings 1887/7 (S Chanderpaul 31*, CEL Ambrose 35*)
Sun, 10 Apr -	day 3 -	England 2nd innings 171/3 (AJ Stewart 62*, GA Hick 52*)
Mon, 11 Apr -		Rest day
Tue, 12 Apr -	day 4 -	West Indies 2nd innings 47/2 (BC Lara 10*, KLT Arthurton 0*)
Wed 13 Apr -	day 5 -	West Indies 2nd innings 237 (82.2 ov) - end of match

MATCH NOTES

Day 4 Day 3 Day 2
• RB Richardson (2) retired hurt on 18* from 32/4 (pulled hamstring)
• CEL Ambrose fined 1000 pounds by the match referee after demolishing his stumps upon his second innings dismissal

Chapter 20

AMUSED IN BELGIUM

It's good to see youngsters enjoying themselves, kicking a football in the street, riding around on bicycles and scooters. Good luck to them.

One boy who caught our attention lived four doors down the road from us. Walking past his house you would hear drums being played. We were glad to be four doors away! The drums were being played by young Dominic Howard. A few years later and after they had played with other local bands and groups, Dominic was joined by two other Teignmouth boys, Matt Bellamy and Chris Wolstenholme who had all been to school together at Teignmouth Community College.

In 1994 the boys became MUSE, now World famous and one of the biggest rock bands around. Local boys done good. Songs like Uprising, Starlight, Knights of Cydonia and Supermassive Black Hole together with incredible live concert performances has propelled them to the top. Brilliant music with dazzling light effects have produced sell out concerts and tours globally.

Dominic plays drums and percussion, Chris is on bass guitar, backing vocals and keyboards, Matt is lead vocal, guitar, piano and keyboards. To give you a flavour of their success, let me highlight. They have sold out Wembley, Madison Square Gardens in New York and numerous top stadia all over the World. They have headlined the Glastonbury Festival twice. They have sold over 20 million albums and won numerous top music awards. Put simply, they are BIG.

But, here's the thing!

These boys are the real deal. A class act who have remained in touch with and loyal to their roots and Teignmouth. They turned up at the Community College just down the road from us, the school they attended as teenagers. They brought a van stacked with musical instruments for the school. What about that.

Teignmouth came to a stop when MUSE put on two sea-front concerts as a thankyou and to share their music with the town. I was not really familiar with their sound, so it was a late decision to get tickets for one of the shows. The Den,

which is a grass area and the focal point by the sea and promenade, hosted the stage and huge crowd. It was a great night and the whole town 'rocked'.

On the walk home after a few drinks Anne and I agreed that the boys coming home like that was great. If they could support us like that then we would reciprocate. I promised Anne we would travel to experience a MUSE concert abroad. Just do it. Get off the bus!

A couple of months later we drove to Dover for the Channel Tunnel. We had a night in Hastings on the way to see our friends Nick and Debbie's son Richard perform in "Joseph" at the White Rock theatre. That was fun and some of the cast joined us for drinks after the show at our hotel next door. The narrator, Tara Bethan, was an absolute darling and having enjoyed her performance it was great to share a drink or three.

She told me about her Dad who had been a boxing promoter. Lovely girl. Richard was in good form. These thespians like to let their hair down after shows. They work and play hard.

Next day through the tunnel and it's 60 miles to Bruges in Belgium for a couple of days in this historical city. It's a canal-based city, the Venice of the North. Beautiful buildings and centre. Then it was another 60-mile drive to Antwerp. We had tickets to a rock concert by a group called MUSE!

Antwerp is the second biggest port in Europe. It's industrial, a working city and it has that feel about it. We found our hotel in the centre which was very modern and fresh. It was near the station so ideal for our evening train to the sports stadium and the twenty-five thousand sell-out. A glass of champagne inside plus memorabilia for friends i.e. t-shirts and caps, then into our seats. They appeared to be behind scaffolding. Well I wasn't having that. An assistant with beautiful brown eyes told me we actually had two of the best seats in the house. Trust me, she said, you will see what happens when the concert starts. Anne and I in our late 50's then were amongst the oldest there. So what. As the show started we were simply blown away.

Three small revolving stages rose through the scaffolding just in front of us rising to around thirty feet right to our height. Each stage had one of the boys with their kit ready to play. We might as well have been on the stage with them. In front the fans were going wild. Our seats were great. Kind of behind the group looking out at the audience. The whole experience was right up there. The music, the atmosphere. Top ten experience, no doubt. Wow. Does it appear we enjoyed it? We did.

Afterwards thousands of us had to get a train back into the city. The queues were unbelievable. Everyone going the same way. It seemed too simple surely to get a train going the other way for one stop before jumping on one coming back. We did and within minutes laughed as we sped past the thronging mass of people. Back to the hotel for drinks. Many MUSE fans filled the bars. We showed our tickets to some youngsters as proof we had been, also spoke about our boy next door Dominic. They loved it.

Finally, I asked why the group was so big in Belgium. Easy, said the fan who was their spokesman. It's because the music is brilliant and they are great guys. Well, there you have it. Easy.

Chapter 21

STAY ON THE BUS – SOUTH AFRICA

The Big Five

Goodness me. South Africa. This could be special. And it was. My school friend Jackie and I had kept in touch for over 50 years. Remarkable when you think about it. Her smile could light up a room and it still does. Just occasionally you meet someone a little bit special. She is. Jackie married Kevin Knowles. We all sat together for English and History lessons. They were always an item and got married to no-one's surprise. We went to their wedding where the entry tune was A Whiter Shade of Pale by Procol Harem. Will never forget it.

Jackie had visited us in Devon a few times and now after years of promises it was our turn to visit her. Knowing of my love of sport she moulded our visit accordingly. We arrived in Cape Town airport and walking along the thoroughfare looking down through the big glass windows the first person I saw was Jackie. Unbelievable. Big smile and a wave. Hello South Africa. My son-in-law Paul, knowing a safari was on the itinerary, had given me one piece of advice. Hey John, safari – "stay on the bus". Nice one.

Jackie lives in Durbanville around fifteen miles from Cape Town on the edge of the garden wine country route. Splendid. Before you could blink it was lunch at her local and then 5 minutes on the road to her nearest wine producing estate. Phizante Kraal owned by the Brink family since 1897. The wine was outstanding as were the cosy lunches they served us on a couple of later visits. We loaded a few bottles and it was back to Jackie's.

With Jackie, welcome to South Africa

Table Mountain, Cape Town

Her house felt safe, but she has alarm pads which connect to an armed guard who drives around on patrol. This is South Africa and there is no denying the underlying tensions. I managed to press one in error. The phone rang right away and Jackie said it was an accident so not to worry. The guard turned up with his rifle a few minutes later anyway in case Jackie was being forced to say all clear! Every house seemed to have a dog for security. Don't think I could live like that. It was worse in Johannesburg. Kevin had been in retail and would drive around his store a few times in the morning before opening up in case of robbers.

We went to Boschendal. The weather was glorious. The estate was stunning. They have different grapes growing in rows for you to inspect. Then we collected a picnic hamper complete with pate, fine bread, jams and cheese. We sat with our wine in the garden and caught up on our families and experiences.

We did the usual tourist visits. The red bus around Cape Town, Signal Hill, The Waterfront, the Olympic Stadium. We drove right around the Cape Peninsula taking in all of the glorious scenery, stopping at the Cape of Good Hope the most South Western point of the South African continent. To be fair, you have to stop or you would drive straight into the ocean! Highlights included Camps Bay overlooked by the twelve Apostles on the Western face of Table Mountain with Lions Head behind. A whole string of beaches down to the Cape and Cape National Park complete with baboons all over the place. Simons Town with its harbour and S.A. Naval presence.

The beautiful Bloubergstrand Beach looks across the ocean on the West Coast to Cape Town and Table Mountain. We walked for miles, blown away by the wonder of it. Back in Cape Town it was third time lucky to go to the top of Table Mountain. The famous table cloth of cloud had made viewing one of the World's wonders impossible for several days but now it was clear. I was a little nervous of the sheer cable car ride to the mountain top while Anne was carefree. I took comfort from the fact that since its opening in 1929 over 22 million people have been taken to the summit. Panoramic views in every direction this World Heritage site with its vegetation and wildlife is truly magnificent. Birds include the redwing starling, chat, swifts, kestrels and the black eagle. On the ground look out for the agama lizard, a variety of snakes, the dassle, like a guinea pig. Apart from the snakes, beware a breed of Chinese tourists who seem to barge around looking for the best vantage points.

Taking a boat from the Victoria and Albert Waterfront to Robben Island, takes around an hour. We went on a cold misty day. As we approached the island the sun burst through and it was glorious. A couple of whales jumped out of the ocean near to us and on the Quay sat hundreds of penguins. It looked pretty but they combined to produce one of the most horrendous smells you will ever have the misfortune to come across!

Nelson Mandela was incarcerated for 27 years, 18 of them on Robben Island. Our guide was a former prisoner who was able to give us an insight to the island and what it was like to be held. Up to 50 men could be held in a single long hut sleeping on mats. Food rations depended on where you were from. African 'Bantu' people got 5 ounces of meat and no jam or syrup as they were grade c class people. Coloureds and Asians got 6 ounces of meat and jam and syrup.

Political prisoners were kept apart. Mandela had his own tiny cell. A hard floor. Caged like an animal with a little table, a plate and bowl. Unexpectedly I found it emotional.

On leaving a dozen or so tourists including us were told the boat was full. We would have to wait 20 minutes for another boat. While waiting one miserable specimen kicked off that it was not good enough having to wait 20 minutes to get off Robben Island. My response to him was simple but to the point. "How do you think Mandela felt?".

NOW, LET'S GET SPORTY!

We will start with a visit to Ernie Els' Wines at Stellenbosch. Ernie is a golfing legend who won our Open Championship in 2002 and again in 2012. He has won tournaments all over the World. He is a big man. Having stood next to him, he seems taller than his given six feet three. A top South African sportsman he is renowned for his effortless golf swing known as the BIG EASY. He has not surprisingly a BIG EASY WINE range. Tasting them and his other Varietals and Proprietors ranges was a pleasure sitting on the patio at his vineyards club house.

The views are spectacular, and he has a solitary golf flag on the lawn as a feature. Inside, his boardroom houses many of his golf trophies and mementos. In addition to our Open he won the US Open in 1994 and 1997 and finished second in the Masters in 2000 and 2004. With 71 professional wins he is one of golf's greats.

Now let's go to Durbanville Golf Club. Jackie had made an appointment for me to meet Alan Dainton, a founder member, who was the club's first captain in 1971. Originally from our Midlands, he worked in the automotive industry before and after he emigrated as a young man. Over a few whiskies, and with great humour, he explained how the club was started and how it evolved.

I asked him about apartheid and he said the club was open to all regardless of colour. It has, however, been always predominantly white because of financial restraint. For some years the club had no liquor licence. That was sorted when a top government official visited to play as a guest. Unable to get a drink he was told of the problem. In true South African politics style, a licence appeared the following week.

The club's Mr Fixit, Wayne, showed me around the course and he was rightly proud of the reservoir he had helped dig and fill for irrigation of the course. With the run of the club, he showed me the kitchens and dining room where a graduation ball was in full swing. Vital income for the club just the same as our own clubs. I visited Wayne's bungalow in a guarded complex. Talking to him and meeting Jackie's friends was so interesting. Their views, as born in South Africa whites, were, shall we just say, rather different with regard to colour, apartheid, politics, Robben Island, Mandela and just about everything else. I will leave it there except to say that Wayne tried to tell me conditions during his National Service army years were worse than on Robben Island. Not buying that one. He also made a point about one man's hero can be another man's terrorist. That's how Mandela was viewed by many in South Africa before the great man, on his release, showed forgiveness beyond belief, going on to lead South Africa and doing good all over the World. Wayne also said he kept a pistol under his pillow!

One thing the locals all agreed on was blade runner Oscar Pistorius guilt in shooting his girlfriend at night in his apartment. On a free day I watched live TV as the verdict came in. Already guilty of manslaughter the state appealed that he be guilty of murder. He was guilty. It was November but he was bailed until April when he would be sentenced for murder. That's justice South African style. Guilty of murder but go home and come back after Christmas! We all agreed you would say to your partner "Did you hear that?" if there was a noise in the night. You would not go to the bathroom and blast away as he did. He had previously had gun related issues in public. "He did not have a leg to stand on" said Wayne along with every third person we met or so it seemed.

THE LONE RANGER ENJOYS CRICKET! – JONATHAN KNOWLES

While staying with Jackie we could not believe it when we saw footage of her son on TV. He is a huge cricket fan and one of the daily papers also carried the story of his visit to see South Africa play a test in a remote part of India at Vidarbha Cricket Ground, Nagpur.

The game started on Anne's birthday, November 25th, as we were flying to Cape Town so we arrived just in time to share the topical news. The newspaper, which I have, wrote the following

THE LONE RANGER

The stadium was filled with Indian fans, cheering and screaming for India. Amid the Jeetega bhai Jeetega India chants one single South African supporter was sitting quietly watching his team's capitulation.

Jonathan Knowles, who loves cricket, has travelled all the way from London for the Test. Before that he has been to Sri Lanka, Dubai and Australia. He had also witnessed the Test match between India and South Africa at Newlands in '96/'97 where Sachin Tendulkar scored a magnificent 169. "I am a thorough patriot. I have been supporting the team ever since I started knowing the game. It's a moment of pride to support your home nation on foreign soil. The feeling is amazing" he told the 'Hitavada'! Like many others he also voiced his discontent with the nature of the pitches. "I think Proteas performance is not impressive as the pitches are more spinner-friendly. I hope the story is different in the next Test in Delhi" He said.

We found time due to Jackie's preparation to call in at a landmark in South African cricket history. This ground was home to the first turf wicket. The field was named 'The Pickstone Oval'. A game was being played and the ground was like so many of our village greens. The sun was shining. We were able to go into the modest club house. Sandwiches were being made. The only give away to the history came from photographs and honours boards adorning the wooden walls. An MCC team that visited in 2000 to play a celebration game honouring the development of the first turf wicket. Games had been played on matting previously. 1964/5 a previous MCC Tour. The Pickstone Oval is at Franschhoek the home of the intrepid Groot Drakenstein Cricket Club. Good luck to the club and teams that visit from all over the World.

We checked out Kenilworth home of Cape Town horse racing. They hold the J&B meet there each year featuring racing followed by a party where glamour is the theme. It attracts 50,000 people.

On to Newlands Cricket Stadium, a 25,000-seater, where South Africa play test matches and Cape Cobra's call home. In the same area Newlands Stadium, a 51,000-capacity arena and home of the DHL Stormers. This is where any rugby-mad South African will call the home of rugby. It was one of the host venues in the 1995 World Cup which South Africa famously won in extra time with Joel Stransky kicking a drop goal. Mandela, as President of South Africa, attended wearing a No.6 Springbok rugby shirt just like captain Francois Pienaar. The game was played at Ellis Park, Johannesburg. With Rugby Union so popular we go now back to the Waterfront to the Springbok Experience. This building houses the history of South African Rugby. It is a treasure chest of photos, blazers, trophies and all manner of memorabilia. Just a few quick one's because we have a safari to go on!

A life-sized statue shows Mandela presenting the rugby World Cup to Pienaar. Wearing the same shirt was a powerful symbol of reconciliation and national unity. Hollywood made the film Invictus to celebrate the event. The Cecil Rhodes Cup was given in 1898 to the South African Coloured Rugby Board. Rhodes, the Englishman, made his money in mining. The Currie Cup was given in 1891 when Sir Donald Currie took the first British Isle team on his ship to South Africa.

> ❝I think Proteas performance is not impressive as the pitches are more spinner-friendly. I hope the story is different in the next Test in Delhi❞

Stay on the bus

Get back on the bus

Chapter 22

SAFARI AND MATJIESFONTEIN

Driving to Aquila Game Reserve for our safari experience I reflected on the contrasts of South Africa. The weather is nice. It's good on the bones. The sun shines. Have a shady place to call home. Sure. But in terms of a way of life it's great if you have money and health. The countryside is truly stunning. The colours remarkable. An oil painter's dream. Against that the townships, the shanty towns and poverty. We drove past and around the shanty towns. We did not want to stop and take a look. In any case Jackie was firm, "Look, if you visited any town in England you would not visit the roughest estate you could find, would you?" "If you went to New York, you would not go to Harlem, would you?" My response was "Well actually we did but I very much take your point".

Arriving at Aquila maybe two hours North of Cape Town it felt good. I had never put a safari high on my list of things to do but now we were here well, bring it on. Tally ho!

We had a lodge with an outside shower. Jackie had the one next to us. It was comfortable. In South Africa they have a big five of animals. Lion, leopard, elephant, buffalo and rhino. Over the course of a few days we saw them all up real close. Well maybe the buffalo was up in a hill but the others, wow!

Our driver was local, and the safari truck was okay in a basic kind of way. At a stop for refreshments in the middle of nowhere I checked out his driving area. I said to him "Where do you keep your rifle?" "Don't carry one", he replied. Paul was right. STAY ON THE BUS!!

We saw ostrich, elephants, springboks, giraffes, hippos. Lots of zebra. Collectively they are known as a dazzle of zebra.

This was clearly a well-organised game reserve. Situated in Touws River, Western Cape, it's an ideal safari location. Especially if you want the experience to be real but not based in a harsh location. We never felt in danger and suspect that the animals are never short of food to keep them together in their own areas. To see these majestic animals of course was a treat. We drove out of the reserve feeling enriched. I indicated to turn left back to Cape Town after breakfast and was taken aback when Jackie said "Hold it. I have a surprise for you. Turn right. We have another two-hour drive in the opposite direction into the wild Karoo semi-desert region". What's going on? Jackie was about to produce what turned out for me to be a sporting and cultural gem. An Aladdin's cave of history, education and fascination. After all we had seen why would a trip into the Karoo Desert in the middle of nowhere end up as a trip highlight? After all, there was nothing there. Or was there?

We drove through the semi desert and up and down highland passes. Eventually we pulled off the main road into what at first sight looked like a railway siding but on closer inspection seemed like a long one street town with one or two smaller roads attached. There was a railway line and station with a bright red English double decker bus parked outside.

Across the road stood an impressive Victorian style hotel. Milners Hotel. A few shops, a garage, an old fire station. A little white church with a few houses. We were in a town I had never even heard of MATJIESFONTEIN pronounced Mikeysfontain. But why were we here?

We started with a drink in Milners Hotel. We were greeted in an empty bar by a Louis Armstrong lookalike, the great American negro jazz singer. He greeted us warmly and then sat at the old bar piano and played and sang us some songs. Bizarre! While it was jovial, the likeness to Louis did not extend to his singing. He could see my interest and showed us around. This included a lounge at the rear of the hotel. On a table sitting with pride of place sat a huge trophy. The inscription made reference to the England Cricket team. What was this all about?

Up the road there was a small motor museum. Pride of place was a Daimler car which was used to carry King George VI, the Queen Mother and a teenage Elizabeth now our Queen and Princess Margaret during a visit to the Cape in 1947. Beneath and behind the rail station we found a museum of more bits of history dating around Victorian times.

Medals, clothing, cricket balls, cameras, dentist chairs, cooking utensils. All manner of things. What did all this mean? Matjiesfontein had a story to tell. I needed to know about all of this. My curiosity was raging. I needed some answers. I got them, and it goes something like this.

In 1877 a nineteen-year-old Scot James Logan arrived in South Africa. He docked at Simon's Town aboard The Rockhampton. He had intended to go to Australia but a storm and damage to the ship saw him decide to stay in South Africa. He was seeking his fortune and like others wanted to join the expansion of the British Empire to do so. The thing about the British Empire and colonisation was straightforward. In essence, and Britain was not alone in this, be bold and brave enough to sail to foreign lands. Once there, put a flag in the soil and claim the land in the name of your ruling King or Queen. You then proceed to develop, rule, exploit, educate to our way of thinking. We will introduce our religion and a variety of ailments you do not have. We will also introduce cricket because without it civilization is lacking. It's just not cricket old boy. And actually, in truth, you may well love it and enjoy it well enough to beat us on occasions. Regardless that you may have been here first in many cases for centuries you have things we want. It's time to rock and roll to our tune baby!

Let's cut to the chase. Logan had worked with a rail company in Scotland, so he got a job with Cape Colonial Railways. At 20 he became Stationmaster at Cape Town Station. He became District Superintendent. The railway was expanding towards the Kimberley Gold and Diamond mines. Logan got the catering rights after his marriage to, the very well connected in Cape Town, Emma Haylett. Clever boy. He bought land, semi-desert land, cheaply around Matjiesfontein. He bored down and found water. Now he was really in business. He planted thousands of fruit trees.

Over the years, after exploiting the railway catering contracts and the need for water both for passengers and the locomotives who needed 250,000 litres to cross the Karoo, Logan added another 3 farms. He was known as the Laird of Matjiesfontein with over 10,0000 acres of land. He built a railway section to get his fruit and farm produce to the main line and onward to market. He developed his water plant to include mineral water bottling it for sale with soda, ginger ale and lemonade. He became a very wealthy man.

His farmhouse which he built at Tweedside was grand and he was a wonderful host. Grand catering and entertainment even in the middle of nowhere saw visits from all over as word got out. He was great friends with Cecil Rhodes, the pioneer businessman who owned most of the Kimberley mining rights. Rhodes became Cape Prime Minister but resigned after a bit of a scandal over the issuing of certain railway catering rights to yes, you've guessed it, his old mate Jimmy Logan.

Logan now realised his own health had greatly improved due to the superb climate. He opened the Matjiesfontein Health Spa. He had built fountains, Milners Hotel, planted trees, London style lights. People began to hear of his paradise in the desert. Word spread. The dry air was a cure.

Logan was innovative. Tweedside had the longest telephone connection in South Africa. He had the first wind powered electric generator and flush toilet. He became an MP in the Cape Parliament.

During the Boar War, the British had up to 10,000 troops around Matjiesfontein. Milners Hotel was used as a military hospital. Logan's fame spread all around the World especially in the UK where his exploits made headlines and the people, parliament and royalty alike were aware of his contributions to the Empire.

Over the years visitors to stay with him at Tweedside included Cecil Rhodes regularly, Lord Randolph Churchill, Rudyard Kipling, Edgar Wallace and Olive Schreiner. Logan had his own visits back to the UK where he was embraced for his loyalty with society accepting him as a bit of a hero. Back at the ranch even Prince Sayyid Ali, the Sultan of Zanzibar, stayed at Matjiesfontein. From one royal to another in 1902 Logan, by royal invitation, attended the coronation of King Edward VII at Westminster Abbey.

Logan had built his own little empire in the desert. The one other thing is he loved cricket. He built a pitch at Matjiesfontein and made a big contribution to South African cricket. Just to give you a flavour of his passion driven not least by his concept of cricket as a symbol of the British Empire read on.

He had made enough money to indulge himself. He therefore arranged some of the earliest matches between England and South Africa. Some were actually played at Matjiesfontein where the hospitality was first class. He was a sponsor who also organized teams. He had a hard side. His fame spread too when the England team made ready to sail home from tour without repaying money he was due. He had the Captain and Manager arrested. During the Boar War he took a South African team to England. It was a success. Conan Doyle, of Sherlock Holmes fame, criticized playing war time cricket. Logan looked on it as a diversion and had he not turned Matjiesfontein over to the British Military?

Logan arranged for George Lohmann the Surrey and England cricketer who had poor health to move to Matjiesfontein. He kind of adopted him and they were friends. He is buried next to Logan. When Hawks England cricket team played a team, Logan selected at Matjiesfontein in 1896 he was in his pomp. The Western Province played there also. He presented the Logan Cup to Rhodesia when England played in Rhodesia. He was conscious of good publicity.

It had been an education. Matjiesfontein has diminished since Logan's death in 1920. However, it has been somewhat revived in recent years and declared as a National Heritage site. Something about the feel of the place and the history touched me. As a people we have explored the World and brought great influence to bear for good and not so good. What do the indigenous people think of us? Again, good and not so good.

I watched England play South Africa at Twickenham yesterday. We won 37-21. The English coach is an Australian, Eddie Jones, who has coached all over the World including a role as assistant or technical advisor to South Africa. Before the game he was asked if South Africa would be up for the Test against England. He said, "You can bet on it mate. For South Africa, England is the big one. The result means more than against any other country. It's all about the history!"

"... It's all about the history! "

Chapter 23

SPORTING ENCOUNTERS

JIMMY GREAVES

Bath City v Barnet. Circa 1978. Not the most appealing of football matches. But nevertheless, I was drawn to Tiverton Park for this evening mid-week match and found myself standing on the terraces. Now in his late 30's Jimmy Greaves was playing for Barnet! The greatest goal scorer of all time. Chelsea, AC Milan, Tottenham Hotspur, West Ham United, England and now Barnet?! It was not the best of games. A Barnet midfield player made a very poor tackle diving in and quite rightly getting sent off. Routine except it was Jimmy Greaves! This was the same player I had idolised at White Hart Lane over a decade ago but clearly a lot of water, or in Jimmy's case alcohol, had gone under the bridge since then. No matter, he was still a sporting hero to me!

For any statistician out there, try these out.	
516 First Division matches (now Premiership)	357 goals
57 England matches	44 goals
25 hat-tricks or more in 25 First Division games.	
Leading goal scorer in 12 of 14 seasons for his club.	
Total in all senior competitions 1957-71	491 goals

Jimmy had lightning speed around the box. His positioning and instinct were uncanny. Very often he passed the ball into the net. His peers considered him to be a brilliant goal scorer and that is praise indeed.

Long after his career finished his character and humour was apparent in his books and TV punditry. I had come across the great Bobby Charlton. His goal against Mexico at Wembley in 1966 must be forever remembered as will his career known all over the World. Anyway, I walked past him in a car park and smiled a little nod of respect. He kind of looked through me with a dour expression. Fair enough. But I was relieved when Jimmy commented that for all his success – 106 caps, European Footballer of the Year, honours galore and a knighthood – does not seem to have made him very happy. It's easier to get a rebate from the taxman than a laugh from Bobby!

GREAVSIE

From one
Goalscorer
to
Another

[signature]

In the eighties 'The Saint and Greavsie' show was popular. Jimmy and Ian St John, ex Liverpool star, bounced nicely off each other with great wit and informed views. Don't you always prefer listening to people who have been there, done it and know what they are talking about. It's why I am suspicious about referees who have never kicked a ball themselves.

So, I am in the Imperial Hotel, Torquay for a sporting dinner and charity auction. Jimmy is the guest speaker. We have a nice table and Jimmy is in full flow. We all love him for the institution he is. All except for a Scottish guy who can't take his drink and tries to be a wise guy interrupting. Jimmy shut him up with "Cor blimey mate, when your mother had you she didn't get much of a result did she?" After the speech I noticed Jimmy go over and shake the guy's hand. Nice touch really. Most of us would have preferred for that particular Jock to have been thrown out. The harbour is just below the hotel.

At the auction I bought a signed montage in a frame complete with a match day programme from Saturday 5th October 1968 costing sixpence. Spurs 3 Leicester 2. One Jimmy Greaves 3 goal hat-trick. All nicely signed and hanging in my office. I also ended up with 2 tickets for Arsenal v Newcaslte for one of the last games at Highbury. Arsenal 1 Newcastle 0. A classic Dennis Bergkamp goal. I took my brother Gary to that evening match and got a ticket apparently for going the wrong way up a one-way street! It was dropped after I wrote a letter of appeal. No photographic evidence or maybe an Arsenal supporter did the review.

Talking to Jimmy afterwards I got him to sign my copy of Greavsie The Autobiography which he did – To John. Be lucky. Jimmy Greaves. I asked him later to sign the book. "But I've already signed it." "Yes, Jimmy but not quite how I wanted". He laughed and signed it again. - From one goal scorer to another, Jimmy Greaves. Well I did play centre forward for Calne Town in the Wiltshire Combination averaging a goal every other game!! Classic!

JONNY WILKINSON

I share a birthday with Jonny and it's the 25th May. Saturday 24th May 2014. It's our birthday tomorrow. An early present. Anne and I have driven up from Devon to Cardiff. We are parked in the central University of Cardiff. We know the University well. It does not seem long ago that we were here for our elder daughter Jacqueline's graduation complete with her Bachelor of Science Degree.

Three years before that we dropped her off for the first time away to start her degree. As we left I had to pull over as the emotion got the better of me. Today would be emotional for a very different reason.

We sat in the car park. We were early but it was also pouring with rain, Cardiff, South Wales style. They say it always rans in Manchester. Try Cardiff sometime!

We were here for a sporting epic. But this was a homage to see Jonny Wilkinson play his final competitive game of rugby in Britain. Wilkinson was bowing out on the eve of his 35th birthday in the Millennium Stadium in the Heineken Cup Final. The big one. The winners become Champions of Europe. This was just Jonny's stage.

He was easily the man of the match. Playing for Toulon the French side defeated Saracens 23-6. Faultless Jonny scored 2 penalties, 2 conversions with kicking from the touchline out of the top drawer and yes, you've guessed, he also dropped a typical Jonny drop goal. It was a privilege to be there to see this icon in the home of Welsh rugby. Aside from his kicking, one moment was magical. He dummied to the left before firing a superb long flat pass to set up the move for Toulon's first try.

Such was the performance and his esteem in the game that when he left the field near the end with victory assured the entire stadium rose in a standing ovation that set the hairs on the back of your neck rise in combination with goose pimples all over. Toulon and Saracen fans gave our Jonny a send off to remember. The French love him and at one point a song went up "Jonny por le President!"

Jonny's place in rugby history is assured. His injury time drop goal winning kick in extra time in the 2003 World Cup Final v Australia is the stuff legend comes from. In Australia too! He was capped 91 times by England. With 1179 points he is our greatest points, conversions, penalties and drop goal scorer of all time. He has been awarded the MBE, OBE and CBE. Stop messing around. Arise Sir Jonny Wilkinson!

One other little memory. We were in Ireland staying in a Waterford hotel. I got up early to watch the touring British Lions in New Zealand. I may have been the only Englishman in the TV room. Our Irish friends together with a Welsh element had the temerity to question why was Jonny selected. It gave me great pleasure to turn from my front row position to state proudly. "Very simple boys – WORLD CUP WINNER!" For the record, 67 points in 6 Lions tests in Australia and New Zealand is pretty useful.

Incidentally I visited Jacqueline a few times in Cardiff. Her hall of residence room in the first year was very basic. She clearly needed a bedside table, so I made her one from various old slats of wood. Needless to say, it was appreciated for the thought but became a bit of a laugh in the hall amongst her friends as it was a bit of a disaster really! I took her for a round of golf on another wet day in Cardiff but managed to slide down a slippery slope getting rather wet and muddy. Jacqueline was in hysterics. What are daughters like? We went to a fine restaurant for a steak supper and ended up for educational purposes in a casino. A little down at the end action was needed so one final spin of the wheel was required.

Okay, let's go for my lucky number and your grandmother's birthday. No.9 duly obliged at 35-1. That was the meal paid for plus a nice supplement to her student funds. Great fun!

GARETH EDWARDS

June 1st, our wedding anniversary. To celebrate I took Anne for a little treat. A couple of days at the Celtic Manor Resort, Newport. Five-star luxury. The Ryder Cup was played here for the first time in Wales 2010. Colin Montgomerie captained Europe to a famous victory over the USA. Graeme McDowell secured the winning point in the final game. The 2010 course was widely acclaimed providing a tough but fair challenge.

Sir Terry Matthews, the Welsh-Canadian business magnate and Wales' first billionaire, made his money as a serial high-tech entrepreneur. He has developed Celtic Manor set in more than 2,000 acres of panoramic countryside into an exceptional venue. Three hotels, three golf courses, spas, health clubs, convention centre and so on. World leaders visited for the NATO summit in 2014. Celtic Manor has been awarded numerous awards including Top Conference Hotel a number of times, 2011 Europe's Golf Resort of the Year, Sports Venue of the Year and so on.

Anne was even more thrilled on hearing I had reserved a table for dinner at the exclusive Michelin starred fine dining option at the resort. Intimate with only around 15 tables it was renowned for many courses nouveau cuisine style. Light delicate dishes aimed at taste sensation rather than volume. My type of food. I explained that it had been a good idea to book as the resort could be busy. "Why busy?" asked Anne. "Well, by a complete coincidence it's the Welsh Open Golf Championship". "Coincidence indeed!" said Anne with a smile.

The Welsh Open that year was sponsored by SAAB and as a SAAB driver at the time and my previous connections with SAAB Finance I also wanted to check out a new model. They have ceased to trade now and what a pity. They were great cars and renowned for reliability and safety. Sir Ian Botham proved that when he famously wrote two off in one day's testing, walking away unhurt twice. He also had one on demo for a few days and in true 'Beefy' style held on to it for a year before getting a polite letter asking for its return!

Sitting down in the restaurant we were looking forward to our dining extravaganza. The small room full of expectant diners. Only the table next to and almost adjoining ours was free. This was rectified when a familiar figure walked in with his charming wife. We might as well have been sharing a table such was the intimacy and closeness of the tables. We nodded and said, 'Good Evening' and then got on with our meals. Sir Gareth Edwards and his wife deserved a little privacy. Besides it was our wedding anniversary.

Anyway, we had most of our courses as did they talking sometimes in English, sometimes in Welsh. Towards the end of the meal and being happy that decorum had been satisfied we all kind of smiled and I said, "It's Gareth Edwards isn't it".

"No, it's not" he laughed in his high-pitched voice. The ice broken we then had a good old chat. Gareth had watched my team The Exeter Chiefs recently in Cardiff and liked their style. He admired their progress, a real success story. The Edwards' live on the coast and he told us when John Toshack was Manager at Swansea the team would train on the beach and stop at his house for a cup of tea. Just John or the team as well I was not sure!

Our wives got on well and were quickly talking grandchildren and so on. It was a lovely little sporting cameo for us but sport aside, the Edwards came across as warm, nice people. Gareth was at the hotel regularly as an Ambassador. He laughed when I told him that a few days before, and it really was a coincidence, that Jensen was sat on my lap as grandchildren do and we watched 'That Try' regarded as the greatest rugby try ever scored by Gareth for the Barbarians against the All Blacks at Cardiff Arms Park in 1973. Almost from their own try line Phil Bennett caught a deep kick. He sidestepped and evaded three tackles before passing to JPR Williams. The ball went to Pullin, Dawes, David and Quinnell beautifully worked up the pitch before Edwards with electric pace took the ball finishing the move with a diving try in the left-hand corner.

Gareth Edwards was a miner's son born in 1947. His all-round sporting skill won him a scholarship to Millfield Public School in Somerset. He was gifted in a range of sports. Athletics, gymnastics, football but above all rugby. The complete scrum half. Quick, strong and with a lightening pass. The complete player.

His career saw him play 195 games for Cardiff scoring 426 points 53 Caps for Wales, 88 points and 10 Caps for the British Lions 3 points. He played in 3 Welsh Grand Slam teams. Gareth became a CBE in 2007 for services to sport. He was knighted in 2015 again for services to sport and for charitable services.

From 1978-82 he was a team captain on BBC's Question of Sport. In 2003 in a poll of international rugby players in Rugby World Magazine, Edwards was declared the greatest rugby player of all time.

In Cardiff at St David's Centre stands a sculpture of Gareth Edwards. He has a rugby ball about to be passed. It is a fitting tribute to one of sport's greats.

We enjoyed the Welsh Open and the Celtic Manor. Pulling a sporting occasion into a break or holiday has become something of a tradition with us!

BOBBY MOORE

1985. Wembley. It's a lovely sunny day. My brother Gary and I have two of the best seats in the house courtesy of the Swindon Town Chairman Brian Hillier. We are near the half way line below the Royal Box. Manchester United v Everton.

I glanced around as you do and sat directly behind us knock me down with a feather there sat our legendary 1966 World Cup winning Captain Bobby Moore. He looked immaculately turned out and every inch the sporting icon he was. Next to him dressed in a royal blue suit was his partner Stephanie. We shook hands and I thanked him for what he had done for the country. A little chat about the match ahead and I introduced him to brother Gary who also shook the great man's hand.

The match ended 1-0 to United with a brilliant bending Norman Whiteside shot. We had a great view of that and an even better view of the incident that the final will be remembered for. Kevin Moran took Peter Reid out at the knees with a diabolical tackle. I can still see it and remember saying to Gary "He's got to go for that". I turned to Bobby who winced and shook his head.

Kevin Moran became the first player ever to be sent off in an FA Cup Final. A little bit of history to add to the mix.

Mind you. There have been worse tackles. My memory takes me back to Edinburgh. I was on a finance training course. With plenty of time to spare I went to see Hearts play Bristol City in a pre-season friendly. The crowd was lively and many of the home supporters were, shall we say, well fueled.

The problem was that no-one had explained to Norman 'Bites your Legs' Hunter that the game was a friendly. The ex-Leeds United and England star now with Bristol City looked down right mean from the kick-off. It came as no surprise when right in front of us and near the touch line he took a Hearts player out at the knees. It was a shocker. Norman started walking off straight away. The red card was inevitable. The crowd went wild with all manner of things including bottles being thrown at him. No coins though. Well, we were in Scotland!

Such was the stature of Bobby Moore that West Ham retired his number 6 shirt.

Bobby Moore OBE played 108 matches for England. He had thirteen seasons at West Ham and six at Fulham. He was a captain who played and led with assurity and command. Pele called him the best defender he played against. He was in 1966 the first footballer to win the BBC Sports Personality of the Year. Rarely in sport and life generally is a person held in such high esteem both as a sportsman and a man. It was an honour to shake his hand.

The trip back was also eventful. Brian Hillier was driving. We had a nice meal only to find his Jaguar had a puncture. Brian, Gary and I were not the practical types to change the tyre which was eventually sorted. It meant we got back to Calne very late for a nightcap at Brian's house. Approaching the garage, the door was open and in the headlights on the workbench sat the biggest rat you can imagine. After building up a bit of courage Brian got out and threw a dustbin lid at it and missed but making one heck of a noise. The rat ran off and the front door burst open. "What's going on" said Beryl, Brian's wife. It was a rat said Brian. "You've been drinking, don't blame a rat" she said. We all laughed and went in for a nightcap.

GORDON BANKS

Tenerife. So. I'm about to play golf once more at Golf Del Sur and Alan says to me "Have you checked who's on the tee ahead of us". Well, I had not taken much notice, but I did now. Gordon Banks was in a three ball. The second player looked like Peter Thompson, the Liverpool and England player and who was in the 1966 world Cup winning squad. Gordon of course was our World Class goal keeper. The third member of the threesome well I've no idea! Something about Golf Dell Sur and Tenerife draws sportsmen in the winter. Alan had played with Terry Cooper, Ex-Leeds and England attacking full back, a few days earlier.

Gordon Banks OBE is 78 now and this was only a couple of years ago so no spring chicken. He played 628 games, 73 Caps for England. His main clubs were Leicester City and Stoke City. Regarded as one of the best goal keepers of all time, he is remembered for 'that save' to prevent Pele scoring in the 1970 World Cup. His career was cut short in 1972 when a car crash cost him an eye. Talking to him, the loss of the eye is evident. He still managed to play a couple of seasons in America. Remarkable.

At Golf Del Sur his threesome had a buggy and two trollies. 6 holes each in the buggy and 12 holes walking. How sensible to take the exercise without over doing it.

On one hole my golf ball went over the green to the next tee where Gordon was waiting for his par three green to clear. I chipped close to the flag from twenty-five yards for Gordon to say, "Great shot". Praise indeed from a legend. After the game I stopped Gordon's taxi from leaving. He or one of his friends had dropped a head cover which I passed into the car and taking the opportunity to shake a great man's hand. It had to be done!

CHRIS KAMARA – EX-FOOTBALLER AND TV PUNDIT

The chap in front of me paying for his round of golf looked familiar. We were at Golf Del Sur, Tenerife again which is a good place to lose some of the winter in England. Sunny and warm rather than wintry and cold works for me. Short shirt and shorts versus pullovers and winter trousers is a no brainer. He turned and beamed as he does on the TV when reporting "How you doing?" he said jovially. What a friendly character.

"I'm fine Chris, by the way, I used to watch you every home game at Swindon Town. You were good" (He was). "That's your team then!" to which I replied "Yes" thinking well, if I'm watching them every week it's not going to be Bristol City is it. Chris still looks trim and in good shape. He was a tough tackling central midfield player with a kind of rolling unique running action. In today's terminology he always 'put in a shift'. For the record his opening drive on the North Course first hole went out of bounds amongst bungalows which skirt the left-hand fairway!

Chris is well liked for his bubbly match reports at Sky Sports. His catchphrase being "Unbelievable Jeff". He has worked on various shows and has presented goals on Sunday since 2000. Well-travelled as a player he made 778 appearances scoring 86 goals. He managed at Bradford City and Stoke with mixed results before going into TV. What a personality. Unbelievable!

RAY REARDON

Doug Walters was a character. He served in the Second World War as a wireless operator in a three-man tank mainly in the middle East. There was a gunner and the tank driver my father. Thrown together as young men life long friendships were formed. For five years they were serving their country. As I wrote earlier, having been abroad for so long my own father on his return never really wanted to travel or leave his home town and family ever again. Many did not want to talk about or relive wartime experiences. In Calne we had one chap who returned and would drop to the floor and curl up shaking. He had been a Japanese prisoner of war and had been through hell.

Doug Walters lived in Torbay and was a keen golfer at Churston Golf Club. Given the history, Doug and I had the odd game and of course, it was great to hear some of the old stories over a lunch helped down with a glass of red wine. My father's favourite was the time when their tank was selected to lead a column through dangerous territory. The front tank was clearly first in line for any attack or land mine. It seems that our intrepid radio operator made contact reporting trouble in communication reception with the radio, so the tank would have to pull over. How the war was won!!

Sitting in the Churston Clubhouse Doug explained that they had a new chef. The old one had been arrested a few days before in the club kitchen. He was on the run from the Police but had still managed to get a chef's job at Churston. So much for background checks and references in those days.

Over lunch, which was most pleasant, a well known and popular figure walked in and was doing the rounds of tables. Our celebrity cut no ice with Doug. We were having a private lunch which Doug cherished. As our celebrity approached Doug looked at him and taking no prisoners said, "Now look, this is a private conversation. Piss off Ray". Everyone laughed including a certain Ray Reardon MBE the six-time World Snooker champion who dominated snooker in the 1970's and is one of the greatest players of all time. Ray became Captain at Churston and came over to Teignmouth to formally open our new pro shop extension. A pleasure to meet Ray, even better spending time with Doug.

Snooker is a tough game to play. When you get on a full-size table you realise how good the pros really are. My friend Nick and I used to play most Thursday nights. Five or six balls down in a row was a miracle!

Anne and I went to the UK Championships in York one year as we were in the area and we noticed the skill and also the number of people coughing. In a quiet room it's almost continuous. Graham Dott was playing and his match was going on late after our planned dinner time. Did Anne want to leave? Not likely, she loved it and dinner became sandwiches and a pint back at the hotel. Hendry, Higgins, White, Davis all come to mind. On his day, Ronnie O'Sullivan probably takes the prize. What a performer. Like most genius he has his issues. Goes with the territory.

CHESTER BARNES

Another time at Churston as Teignmouth Captain and saying a few words on behalf of our team I reminded their Captain that we had played table tennis when he was giving exhibitions circa 30 years ago at Butlins Holiday Camp, Bognor Regis. I was a dining hall porter on a school summer holiday job. He was one Chester Barnes, England Champion and number one player in the 60's and 70's. I had a pale blue coat on and Chester said he did not remember our game all those years ago but he did remember the coat!

SIR NICK FALDO

We drove up to Scotland in 2009 for the Scottish Golf Open at Loch Lomond. I suggested doing a little missionary work, but Anne felt sure that most of our Scottish friends were now firmly in the 21st century. I reminded Anne of that comment as our journey up took us through the Gorbals, an area on the South Bank of the River Clyde in the City of Glasgow. Over time it had become over populated after being badly affected by industrialization. People could not afford their own homes and it became widely known as a dangerous slum associated with the problems of drunkenness, drugs and crime. Stay on the Bus! In recent decades much of the area has been demolished and re-developed but the stigma remains.

We drove through Parkhead taking a quick look at Celtic Park, the home of Celtic Football Club. Celtic famously became the first British team to win the European Cup

in Lisbon 1967. 25th May to be precise! Celtic in their green and white kit became known thereafter as the Lisbon Lions, beating Inter-Milan 2-1 with goals from Tommy Gemmell and Stevie Chalmers. Jock Stein's Celtic played an attacking style in contrast to the Italian's defensive set-up typical of Italian teams.

We stayed in Tarbet, a small village in Argyll and Bute on the banks of Loch Lomond. Our accommodation was superb with the most wonderful panoramic views up the Loch. Diane and Alan had driven up in their camper and were in a field nearby almost close enough for me to see from my in room jacuzzi. Give me hotel comfort any day!

We walked to the local Bay Tarbet Hotel one evening for a pint or two. It had a Saga crowd in with several buses outside. I am not saying they were old, but the comedian stopped his act several times to allow a toilet comfort break! The Police had a road check block going. Something to do with a drug run to Glasgow with a few drink drivers thrown in. We walked the few hundred yards to our hotel. Diane and Alan got a taxi back to their field/camp site.

Loch Lomond Golf Club is blessed with natural beauty. The Loch, complete with a mixture of boats, the splendid scenery, the mansion house, birds singing, idyllic really and then Colin Montgomery came into view with his trademark scowl. When he is over a ball woe betide anyone who moves or actually, anyone thinking of moving. Good job he does not carry a gun! He might have used it many times over the years. You get the impression no-one would be safe. Now let's be fair to Monty, you don't have his career without being driven and determined. Eight European Tour Order of Merits, Ryder Cup Captain, unluckiest player not to win a major, MBE, OBE. I admire his swing greatly. Makes up his mind, moves and plays quickly with a lovely rhythm. He has won Senior Tour majors and is also doing commentary which he can do well with when he gets more fluent and drops his er and ah. Bit like Arsene Wenger with his well aah, I aah, I did not see it.

We watched the players on the practice putting green. Some practiced alone while others had their caddy and coach in attendance. They drifted away until only one player remained. It did not surprise me that the last man standing was our greatest ever golfer. Then aged 52 and firmly in the twilight of his tournament appearances, this icon was I suspect having fun complete with his son on his bag. Probably a little rusty from lack of play he still wanted to be as good as he could be. He was not realistically expecting to win this week, but pride would dictate an acceptable effort. Calling it a day he strode towards us.

"Congratulations on the knighthood Nick", I said. He stopped and said "Thanks". It was only now stood next to him I realised what a big bear of a man he is. Early career photos show him as a lean lithe young man. Now I am 6-foot-tall but Nick, as the photo Anne took shows, loomed over me. I told Nick a photo would be good for my office wall and he said words to the effect "Fine, good idea".

Anne lined us up and I said to her "Get this right or we are in divorce territory". Nick turned and gave me a knowing look. After three divorces I maybe was straying into familiar territory for him. We had a little chat and it was great to meet him. The next day we were behind the ropes. He looked across and gave me a nod. I don't think he misses very much. A man you would want next to you.

Sir Nick Faldo was born in Welwyn Garden City, Hertfordshire in 1957. He turned professional in 1976.

PGA Tour wins - 9
European Tour wins – 30
3 Masters Tournament wins 1989, 1990, 1996
3 Open Championship wins 1987, 1990, 1992

Nick won numerous awards including European Tour Order of Merit, Golfer of the Year, PGA Player of the Year, BBC Sports Personality of the Year.

Nick was reputably not the most popular player among his peers. So what? His Ryder Cup Captaincy was not best received. So what? In my eyes, Nick Faldo is a sporting hero. His achievements transcend others and I give him plenty of slack where criticism from others is concerned. His grit and single mindedness set him apart. What a Champion.

Nick was a key player in four winning Ryder Cup teams. He has made more appearances and won more Ryder Cup points than any other player from Europe or the USA. Not only the best and most successful golfer of all time from Britain, the great Jack Nicklaus, who inspired Nick to play golf, puts him among the greatest players ever to have walked the World's fairways. Praise indeed.

Since taking up golf, Nick has dedicated himself to being the best golfer he could be. English Amateur Champion in 1975, he was professional by 1977 and had wins each year including the Sun Alliance PGA Championship in 1980 and 1981, the French and Swiss Opens in 1983, the European Order of Merit in 1983. In the USA a first win at the Sea Pines Heritage in 1984. But Nick was not happy. He wanted to win majors. He was mixing with the best players and doing okay but that was not enough for a man seeking to be the best.

In 1984 he came 55th in the US Open, 15th in the Masters, 6th in the British Open and 20th in the US PGA. A good living but he wanted to get to the next level. So, he did a remarkable thing. He basically got together with the coach David Leadbetter and started again working on a new swing. Effectively he was in the wilderness for 1985/86 determined to reach a level that could put him with the elite. His dedication was unbelievable. His gamble paid off though and he came out smiling with those six majors between 1987 and 1996 including back to back Masters in 1989/90. He took another gamble taking on unusually a lady caddy, Fanny Sunesson. They made a good team. He viewed her not just as a bag carrier but as a personal assistant on the course. And he was muted to have said light heartedly, "Well, even if I don't win I still have Fanny". More to the point he was impressed by her professionalism and had seen her in action on their circuit. As I noted earlier, I don't think he misses very much.

In 1987 Nick won his first major. The Open Championship at Muirfield, Scotland. In stormy weather he played remarkably. The final round in a cool misty climate is widely acclaimed. He parred every hole to claim victory. He won again here in 1992. Winning the Open at St Andrews in 1990 the home of golf, was icing on the cake. All the greats want to win at St Andrews. Jack Nicklaus, like Nick, counts victory at St Andrews among their crowning achievements. Course they do!

Nick Faldo is now a legend on USA TV. He commentates with knowledge and good humour. His character and wit go down well in the States. Maybe far better than in the UK where perhaps he has not really been understood. A complex, driven man but a true sporting great.

STEVE BOYLE

One of the benefits of working in the finance industry was that you got to meet and work with a whole variety of colourful people. Some real characters. When Manager of Lloyds Bowmaker in Bristol I was given a new assistant. Enter Steve Boyle. Steve was a big lad. Broad shoulders with a nose that had probably been broken a few times he had the aura of a guy not to be messed with. On getting to know him he was jovial and good to have around.

We would sometimes go to the sports club opposite our Queens Square office in the heart of the city. Steve would work out the weights while I had a quiet pint. He would call me 'Boss' which I never liked. "Steve, it's John not boss". "Okay John understood". A couple of minutes later it would be "Right, I'm off now, see you in the morning Boss"! He would set off back to the hotel he owned up the road near Gloucester. I never quite worked out which was his 'proper' job, and which was part-time. Steve had a good sense of humour and in fairness when in work he pulled his weight which was considerable.

Have I not mentioned that Stephen Brent Boyle was also an England International Rugby player who toured with the British Lions to New Zealand in 1983. He was a lock forward who played 312 games for Gloucester scoring 77 tries. He was well known for powerful scrummaging and his ability at the front of the lineout.

Steve played in two Twickenham Cup Finals. I had been to one of them in 1978. A dour, tough match. Gloucester beat Leicester 6-3 and Steve gave the pass to Richard Mogg for the winning try. He finished his rugby with Moseley.

Steve was modest at work about his fine rugby career which had now ended. It was before the professional era as such. Players no doubt were helped by their clubs, expenses could be stretched but basically, they needed a career. Ideally one where any employer made allowances for training or tours. I asked Steve to bring his ties, shirts and medals in to show the staff, but he would just say they were in a drawer somewhere and leave it at that.

Funnily enough while writing this book a few days ago and purely by coincidence looking at the holiday pages it seems that The Pilgrim Country House Hotel near Ross-on-Wye, Hertfordshire is owned and run by one Steve Boyle, a former England and Lions rugby player. It's a fun hotel on a hill with sweeping views of the Black Mountains and the Brecon Beacons National Park. Steve apparently has been at the hotel for a decade. Rates are reasonable, and the 20 rooms are simply decorated yet smart. A great base for walkers next to the Herefordshire Trail. No charge for the plug Steve, keep changing the sheets!

Chapter 24

WHAT GOES ON TOUR STAYS ON TOUR

EXACTLY!

So, rest easy boys. Football pre-season tours to Jersey, Devon, Cornwall and Liverpool will remain as tour memories. Golf trips to Ireland, France and other destinations are equally left with selective memory syndrome. Thanks for the memories, laughs and good company.

Chapter 25

WHISKYFIED

At a routine annual checkup and the usual tests, Dr Keane looked me in the eye. All was well, but he wanted to know if I enjoyed a drink. Guilty as charged your honour.

What do you drink?

"Well, beer and wine but in particular I enjoy a whisky in the evening. A few good glasses and I am relaxed. Everything feels as it should".

"Do you drink whisky every night?" he asked.

"Yes".

He looked at me knowingly peering over his glasses and said "So do I!" Priceless.

Well, that's alright then. If its okay with my doctor its okay with me. No need for a second opinion on this one. Anne reckons she can tell if she thinks its one too many. "You are getting whiskyfied" she will state. Has she invented a new word? Can one be whiskyfied due to whiskyfication?

On a visit to the Glenfydich Whisky Distillery in Scotland I discovered the following. Whisky is really Scottish Spring Water. Beautiful spring water. Sure a few ingredients are added but I'm actually drinking spring water! Also, did you know whisky contains only a trace of sugar unlike say a pint of beer which can contain circa seven teaspoonfuls equivalent of sugar.

So yes, I enjoy a drink and don't forget the 19th hole at the golf club provides much needed income as well as an ideal end to a round for friends to chew the fat about the round, the shots left on the course, the putts, shot of the round and anything else that comes to mind.

One no go area for me and it's a strict one. I have never taken a drink before or during sport. I fail to see how it cannot impact on your timing and reactions. Some may like a drink for calming or dutch courage. But show me an opponent taking a drink before a match and you have an advantage. I saw it before a men's Summer

Four Ball Final. We won on the 18th. Did the pint an opponent had affect his play on the first few holes? Who knows.

Brian Barnes is a golfer who was a fine player. He won the Senior British Open and famously beat Jack Nicklaus twice on the same day in the Ryder Cup. Only he could tell you if he would have won more in his career if he had curtailed his legendary drinking.

Drink can be part of social enjoyment, relaxing and helping a party along. It affects people in different ways. When I've had enough it's bed time. Others start nodding after a couple. Some become loud and boorish. A few become argumentative, even aggressive. Over time you know if you have any sense where you fit and what fits you! Some become funny and cast-off inhibitions. Let's be fair, most sportsmen enjoy a beer after a game. It can help team spirit, camaraderie, the crack. Just be in control. I still smile at the footage of Freddie Flintoff staggering out of No.10 Downing Street after an Ashes Series victory. He was wasted!

Where would we be without our pubs. They are part of our culture. A pint in your local is one of life's pleasures. So, enjoy a drink. Don't feel guilty about it. Sir Kingsley Amis, the novelist and renowned drinker, summed it up quite nicely when he wisely expressed that "No pleasure is worth giving up for the sake of two more years in a geriatric home at Weston-super-Mare."

When a non-drinker gets up in the morning that's as good as he or she is going to feel all day. The rest of us know that a little drink later on will be nice. A little reward to help things along.

At a recent Sunday lunch at Sidmouth Golf Club with our friends Chris and Fran Rowe, I mentioned to Chris about the Dr Keane and whisky episode. Chris had a similar chat with his doctor who picked up that Chris also likes a drink. They were talking about levels of drinking. His doctor said, "Do you know the definition of an alcoholic?" "No", said Chris. "It's where you drink more than your doctor. You don't, so you are not!" My definition of depression – An empty wine cellar!

Before the breathalyzer and most of us wised up. I had a good day at Knowle Golf Club. A good charity golf event which went well into the night. It was probably not the best decision to drive back to the hotel. This was confirmed the next morning when I was asked on reception, "Excuse me sir, do you drive a SAAB? We were wondering why you parked it on the lawn outside the hotel main entrance door rather than in the car park?"

On another occasion I am sad to report a finance annual conference evening meal and heavy session. Woke up in the night and went to use the bathroom. The beer had caught up. Basically, I used the wrong door which shut behind me. Now I'm stood in the corridor on the fourth floor. Two problems here. Firstly, in order of importance, I still need to take a jimmy riddle. Secondly, I'm stood locked out with only a pair of pants on. Executive decision easily taken. Into the lift, down to reception. The night porter did not blink. "Happens all the time sir. At least you've got your pants on. A guy last week did not. He got out of the lift just in time to welcome a coachload of German tourists arriving from the airport! Let me get you another key!"

Pete Robinson and I spent a day at the races in Newton Abbot. I was hosting a company race day for customers. Pete came along for a freebie. Pete had invited me to so many functions when he was the secretary at Teignmouth Quay, I went to so many do's people must have thought I worked there. Peter, along with Jeff and Cyril Boyne were good company and hosts.

The races went well. As we sponsored a race I was asked down to the paddock for one race to pick the best turned out horse. Well I can tell you where the horse's head is but that's it so on reflection I gave it to the best-looking stable girl's horse! A long day and a visit to the pub opposite the station meant we got on the train in building terms plastered. On getting into Teignmouth between us we could not work out how to open the train door. Next stop Dawlish. At this rate we could end up in Bristol. Fortunately, an old lady took pity on us and opened the door.

Another visit, on the occasion of Paul's stag do, it was off to the races. We all agreed to meet in the Grandstand Pub by the course. Pete was a no show, a good hour late. The mobile rang. He had gone into the course and was waiting for us in the Grandstand!!

Cheers!

One time I should have had a drink. Alan Booker, my valued colleague, and I had a photo shoot with the actual Lloyds Black Horse. We stood in a field. The Black Horse ran closely past us flat out. That's scary to have a horse running in full flow at you to get to its travelling companion its friendly donkey across the field. Guess what. It had a white nose which was blackened before the shoot!

Another drink involved Richard Armitage, a friend and stalwart at Teignmouth Golf Club. 'Armo' came to my house one evening to discuss business. He has a very successful financial services company in Torbay. He wanted me to join him or sell me a policy or both. I put a bottle of whisky on the table for me and a bottle of gin for him. The evening went well. We remembered the only game of football we had played together for Teignmouth at Totnes. He got sent off! We talked for a good few hours. Golf, finance, you name it. No business was done but we agreed to play in the Club Summer Four Ball together. Next day I inspected the bottles. Only a little left in Armo's gin and the same with my whisky.

Armo rang the next day to recap what we had agreed and laughed. He was a 2 handicap County player one of if not the best player at the club while I was off an 18 handicap. Actually a mix like that can work. We went through the summer winning some good matches knocking out some good pairings before reaching the final. We won on the 18th hole beating Messrs Parker and Sydenham, both previous captains. The pairing continued for many years until Armo's son, Charlie, came of age and they naturally teamed up.

Armo is one of life's characters. He would do you a good turn if he could. A good listener, which is an asset in business, he has a quick wit and a sense of humour which can be misinterpreted by lesser mortals. At Torquay Golf Club he won a trophy and, in his speech, somehow called the course there a track. He was banned by the blazers who had a humour bypass and took offence.

Armo's stag do was interesting. A group of us flew to Dublin for golf, Guinness and a couple of nights on the town. Fancy dress was the order of the day, so I flew as a vicar with appropriate dog collar included. Doors were opened and heads bowed in respect. I fear our air hostess smelled a rat when offering tea or coffee but being asked for a few Bells whisky miniatures instead. At the check-in a stern customs lady asked Armo's country of birth. She thought he was being a wise guy when he said Uganda and sent him to the back of the line. Actually, it was true. Mr Armitage senior was working there at the time.

An earlier golf trip journey to the airport was delayed badly by an accident. We were going to miss the flight. Our action man was out of the coach in a flash and thumbed a lift on a motor bike to get to the airport and hold the flight. Half an hour and a few miles later there he was on the side of the road. The motorcyclist had got near the accident. With no crash helmet Armo had to get off pronto. Word had got through anyway and the flight was held up for us. We got there!

Don't you love the Irish ways of talking. Our bus driver stated

"If you had not come I would not have met you"

"If we were going the other way you would be getting wet"

There's logic in there somewhere!

So, we have been to the Orestone Manor Hotel and Restaurant today for lunch. 25th November 2016. Anne has her birthday on the same day each year. Little bit of Irish logic there. Our eldest daughter Jackie has treated her mother and father to a splendid fine wine and dining experience. Anne enjoyed her chocolate brownie dessert complete with a piped Happy Birthday message in rich chocolate emblazoned across the plate. Nice touch.

Rather than a dessert and not uncommonly I opted for a pint, usually of bitter but on this occasion lager because a gentleman had been served one earlier and it looked invitingly tempting.

Jacqueline surveyed the scene and knowingly said "Enjoy it Dad. The truth is we all like a drink in this family. It's not your fault. It's genetic". Wise words indeed. Such a clever girl.

> " Enjoy it Dad. The truth is we all like a drink in this family. It's not your fault. It's genetic. "

Chapter 26

COWBOYS

So here is the thing and keep it confidential. I have a love of cowboy films. With over 300 in my collection mainly from the 50's and 60's when they peaked, they are pure escapism. I am there with them on the open range, on horseback watching for rustlers, Indians or whatever happens next. The scenery is often spectacular whether we are in monument valley, out West on the plains or in the Rockies prospecting for gold. I am with them in the saloons where a glass or two of whisky is mandatory. And as they say, "Give me the good stuff you keep under the bar!"

The odd observer may be thinking how sad, poor chap. Well forget it, when you spent Saturday mornings at the local cinema watching Messrs Wayne, Scott, Peck, Lancaster, Stewart and so on, you were hooked. One gentleman said to me quite recently "But surely cowboys were for boys who missed out on girls?" Forget it buster, plenty of time for both and not a bad combination!

I was born in 1952 and also that year, in no particular order, The Queen had her coronation and Fred Zinnemann directed 'High Noon' with Gary Cooper. The other thing with cowboys is the tremendous musical scores. High Noon is a point well made and what about 'The Big Country' theme by Jerome Moross. Outstanding.

" But surely cowboys were for boys who missed out on girls "

JOHN WAYNE

37 USA

2004

© 2003 USPS

CLASSICS

JOHN WAYNE	The Man who Shot Liberty Vallance • Chisum Red River • The Searchers • Honcho • McLintock The Commancheros • The Sons of Katie Elder True Grit • The Alamo. (The Quiet Man • McQ great, non-cowboys).
KIRK DOUGLAS	Man Without a Star • Gunfight at the OK Corral The Big Sky (Spartacus and The Vikings non-cowboy classics).
CLINT EASTWOOD	Unforgiven • Paint your Wagon • Joe Kidd The Good, The Bad and the Ugly (Dirty Harry Series Classic)
JAMES STEWART	Destry Rides Again • Winchester 73 • The Far Country Where the River Bends • Naked Bend The Man from Laramie
RANDOLPH SCOTT	Tall Man Riding • Ride the High Country Commanche Station • The Tall T • Santa Fe Abeline City • The Bounty Hunter • Trail Street
BURT LANCASTER	Gunfight at the OK Corral – Lawman • The Unforgiven The Kentuckian • Ulzanas Raid
ROBERT MITCHUM	Young Billy Young • River of No Return
ALAN LADD	Shane
ERROL FLYNN	Dodge City • Virginia City • Santa Fe Trail
GREGORY PECK	The Big Country
HENRY FONDA	The Return of Frank James • Drums along the Mohawk
GARY COOPER	High Noon • Distant Drums • The Plainsman
LEE MARVIN	Monte Walsh
PAUL NEWMAN	Butch Cassidy and the Sundance Kid • Hombre
RICHARD WIDMARK	The Way West
JOEL MCCRAE	Wichita • The Oklahoman • Ride The High Country
CLARK GABLE	The Tall Men
WILLIAM HOLDEN	The Wild Bunch
GLEN FORD	The Fastest Gun Alive • Cowboy
TYRONE POWER	Jesse James
SPENCER TRACY	Broken Lance • North West Passage

House of Commons

Wednesday 26th February 2003

Summary Agenda

11.30 a.m.	Prayers.
Afterwards	Private Business (*without debate*).
	Oral Questions to the Secretary of State for International Development.
12 noon	Oral Questions to the Prime Minister.
12.30 p.m.	Urgent Questions, Ministerial Statements (if any).
Afterwards	Needle Stick Injury—Motion for leave to introduce a Bill under the Ten minute rule (Laura Moffatt) (*for up to 20 minutes*).
	Iraq (Motion) (*may continue until 7.00 p.m.*).
At the end of the sitting	Adjournment Debate: The Council of Europe and the EU Convention on the Future of Europe (Mr David Atkinson) (*until 7.30 p.m. or for half an hour, whichever is later*).

Sitting in Westminster Hall

Adjournment Debates:

9.30 a.m.	Government policy on refugee benefits (Mr Peter Lilley).
11.00 a.m.	Area Based Initiatives in Cornwall and Scilly (Andrew George).
2.00 p.m.	Small businesses and the UK economy (Mr Iain Luke).
3.30 p.m.	Public accountability in Wales (Llew Smith).
4.00 p.m.	Health Fit process and the Isle of Wight (Mr Andrew Turner) (*until 4.30 p.m.*).

Main Business

[*Until 7.00 p.m.*]

2 IRAQ

The Prime Minister
Mr Secretary Prescott
Mr Chancellor of the Exchequer
Mr Robin Cook
Mr Secretary Straw
Mr Secretary Hoon

Michael Fabricant   Peter Bottomley

That this House takes note of Command Paper Cm 5769 on Iraq; reaffirms its endorsement of United Nations Security Council Resolution 1441, as expressed in its Resolution of 25th November 2002; supports the Government's continuing efforts in the United Nations to disarm Iraq of its weapons of mass destruction; and calls upon Iraq to recognise this as its final opportunity to comply with its disarmament obligations.

...cates Government Business.

Chapter 27

WHERE ARE YOU TAKING ME FOR MY BIRTHDAY

Many years ago my father, John Senior, took me to the Savoy Hotel in London as his guest. It was the Road Haulage Association's Annual Dinner. As a transport director with C&T Harris he had a real interest. I recall a nice dinner in the palatial grand dining room. Copious bottles of wine. These boys liked a day out. Now my sense of humour goes in different directions and what followed appealed to my sense of seeing the funny side of a disastrous attempt for example of a speech. This one was right up there.

This card is always good for a laugh when paying a restaurant bill !

The guest speaker was the New Zealand Ambassador who touched on the economy in general and transport in New Zealand before moving on to his special subject. Sheep. Twenty minutes of humourless statistics and dribble had these hardened hauliers counting, well sheep of course. Looking around the room half of them were asleep. There were as many heads on tables as bottles of wine. The odd sheep shagging story might have helped. You know a Welshman when asked what his partner said the first time he had sex ba ba ba and so on. But no, this guy was dire. He got a round of applause because the boys were relieved he had finished!!

15th November 1979. By way of a thank you, and knowing of our mutual interest in politics, I got tickets to parliament and we had a great day out. He was thrilled to be there and cherished being in the House of Commons for the day. We took in a West End show in the evening.

Another trip to parliament was special as Anne and I met the Prime Minister Ted Heath. He was walking in the hall between the chambers, House of Lords and House of Commons. He spotted us and, for reasons only known to him, came over for a chat. He wanted to know where we were from and offered to sign our order paper for the day's events and itinerary. Then came the surprise. He left us, walked into the House of Commons as we took our seats in the strangers gallery and he proceeded to give a major speech. "The Queen's speech on Rhodesia". We were blown away by how calm he had been only minutes before a big challenge. Perhaps it helped to relax him.

This is not a political opinion narrative, so I will not comment unduly on Ted taking us into Europe except to write that it was intended to be primarily a trade agreement. A common market. Since then and over decades various parties have betrayed us big time. It's time to tear up a few treaties methinks. Immigration numbers, human rights. Let's get back to running the country ourselves instead of being run by the Brussels gravy train. I've been over and had a look around it. It's a gin palace!

Margaret Thatcher, when she was PM, visited Calne and went to an engineering company. We got to meet her briefly, but my memory of the day concerned Dennis Thatcher smoking in the factory reception area. With nowhere to put his cigarette butt I observed as he slyly put it in the reception flower display!

Fiona asked me where I was going to take her for her twenty-first birthday. A rather special day was called for. Let's go its Dad and Daughter trip to London, February 26th, 2003.

I arranged tickets to the House of Commons from our local member of parliament at that time, Richard Younger Ross. A little bit of luck because February 26th was to be a very major day in our country's history. The Iraq Debate. Prime Minister, Tony Blair, had to present a major speech the case for our further endorsement of the

United Nations Security Resolution 1441 and the need to disarm Iraq of its weapons of mass destruction.

A jam-packed house. Tension, debate, history in the making and riveting stuff. Looking down from the gallery you really did feel part of it and actually, you were. It's not a big chamber and you are right on top of it all. What a pity that a glass barrier now exists because some idiot threw a box of powder onto the MPs below. The contents were harmless but the threat was real, so the authorities felt security needed to be tightened.

We took in a fair amount of the debate. It all sounded so viable at the time. Events of course and looking back with hindsight raise so many questions. Just where was the evidence? Was Tony Blair being led blindly by President George Bush Junior in awe of the USA? Not Blair's finest hour.

Fiona was now content with her time spent listening to the debate. She did not want to overdose in politics so onwards to our next venue.

A little stroll out of parliament, past Big Ben and over Westminster Bridge. A few yards to the left and it's the London Eye also known as the Millennium Wheel. This huge ferris wheel rising 443 feet is now very much a London land mark. Since its public opening in 2000 at the time being the largest ferris wheel in the World and the highest public viewing point in London it has become a major tourist attraction. Each of its 32 capsules or pods weigh 10 tons and can carry up to 25 people. Each turn of the wheel or revolution takes 30 minutes. Plenty of time to take in the panoramic views. Now after a little spin so to speak, off to venue 3.

Now Fiona loves all things Bond. James Bond 007. Even her wedding reception saw each table with a Bond Theme name. My father of the bride speech started with the Bond signature theme tune music complete with pistol in hand. Well you have to go with the flow!

So, after the London Eye it was off across town to a major James Bond exhibition. Fiona loved it. The Goldfinger Aston Martin DB5 as driven by Bond. The 1937 Rolls-Royce Phantom III as driven by Odd Job for Goldfinger himself. A vast array of footage, vehicles, props, clothing. Really good fun. I especially liked obtaining a spoof James Bond credit card which I have enjoyed presenting at restaurants and shops for many years since. Usually gets a laugh.

After a special day out, we drove back to Devon finding time to stop in Wiltshire and to take Fiona's Grandma Desna for a nice meal once more at the George Inn, Sandy Lane. Happy 21st!

Chapter 28

FINANCE SHORTS

So what? The thing about one's career is that unless you have done something spectacular, who cares! With that in mind let me be remarkably brief.

Left school and went to teachers training at Borough Road College, London under the Heathrow Flight path. Halls of residence room next to the main boiler. Hot! Maggie May was played endlessly in the Union Bar most nights. Didn't like it, exams looming so I left. Over and out. Repaid my student loan. Joined Lloyds Bank, Melksham. Looking for a friendly face I walked in and reported for duty on day one to Anne, who was a rather attractive cashier complete with the fashion of the time. The mini skirt! Following her upstairs lunchtime to the rest room became the highlight of the day. We got married. Several branches later, Salisbury and Chippenham to be precise, I didn't like it. Banking exams looming I left. The final straw was when I was called into the Deputy Manager's office who told me my cashiering and application was good, so he thought I deserved more responsibility. He gave me the keys to the stationery cupboard! Goodnight!

Next stop Uncle Phil got me a trainee accountant job at Westinghouse Brake and Signal Company, Foundry Lane, Chippenham. Complete disaster, help. Starting at 8 and putting printed sheets into ledgers with handwriting. The definition of boredom. By 8.30, and looking up at the huge clock, you felt you had been there all day. Accountancy exams due, didn't like it. Au Revoir. Adios, Addio, Adeus, see you later. MUCH LATER!

The only good thing about it had been good friends made such as Mike Smith and his wife Mel. He was a good footballer and we have kept in touch for forty years. A reunion in Tenerife and a few meals have been great fun.

The next couple of months saw a quickly aborted attendance at Southampton flirting with another accountancy course. You know the story by now. Exams due, didn't like it. Bye bye. Something needed to happen. We had a rather nice flat in Calne with fine views from the centre of town towards the Wiltshire Downs and the famous Cherhill White Horse. Anne had her bank income, but I was kind of floundering. In those days you could easily get another job unlike today I suspect. I needed a break

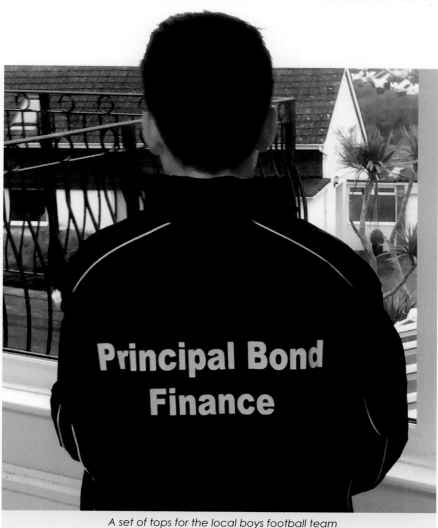

A set of tops for the local boys football team

to find my niche. I got one. Just in time really. Anne asked her bank manager for a loan to buy a washing machine. He laughed and said he would give her a loan to buy a house pointing her in a better direction. I needed to pull my finger out. I did, finding a niche I have been in for forty years. Keep the faith boys and girls!

I joined Lloyds and Scottish Finance and had a good successful career. Starting as a representative in Swindon before promotions to manage branches at Newport, Exeter, Reading and finally Bristol. Along the way the name changed to Lloyds Bowmaker with the merger/takeover of the Bowmaker Group. Someone was paid a lot of money to come up with the name Lloyds Bowmaker!

A few years followed in Agricultural Finance before setting up my own family run finance brokerage which has been fun for circa twenty years now. There, that was not too painful. I would like to share one or two little stories and characters met along the way.

Chapter 29

LLOYDS AND SCOTTISH FINANCE

Edinburgh was the Head Office. The training centre was at Ramsey Lodge next to the castle. Arriving on the overnight sleeper from Bristol into Waverly Station trust me, is grim. A cold mist with Edinburgh's bleak stone buildings. Can't stand the place probably because I think of enforced periods of work under pressure and being away from home.

A customers day at North Wilts Golf Club

The first journey saw me share a two-bunk carriage with another trainee, Chris. After a few cans of lager, I got into the top bunk. Chris went to get into his but pulled down the cover to reveal a sheet with blood all over it. Chris summoned up his feelings with language you would not use in conversation with the vicar. He called for the night porter. An old Northern craggy guy turned and explained the train was full. There was no spare linen. "Leave it to me" he said, following up under his breath with what sounded very much like "Soft southern b******s". He bent down and turned the offending sheet over. Disgusting. "Best I can do tonight lads" and off he went. I was in hysterics. Chris was staggered and spent the night in a seat in the main carriage!

One evening the dozen or so trainees were joined for dinner in the lodge by John Little, the MD, top dog. Sherry in the lounge. We each had to go forward and shake his hand in front of the fireplace and introduce ourselves. One guy who was smoking a pipe found himself holding the pipe and glass of sherry in one hand, so he could shake Little's hand with the other "Richard David from Swansea Mr Little". "Don't you like your sherry Mr David? You are pouring it over my shoes". And he was.

The Branch Manager at Swindon was Andrew Bunting. A dedicated slight man, his worked consumed him. He lived for it and was good at it. Working together for 4 years led to a lifelong friendship. I still miss him. We had some laughs.

The objective was to provide finance to companies in all sectors. I had most of Wiltshire South of Swindon to go at. Park the car and go around industrial estates cold or by appointment. Some days Andrew would come with me and we would take it in turn to lead the call. At Worton Coaches, last call of the day, it was cold and had started to snow. The owner who ran some dozen coaches was lying under a coach in the repair pit. Andrew had said "Leave this one to me John". Andrew peered into the pit and said, "Excuse me". The guy had not seen Andrew and I approach. He was surprised and startled. He brought his wrench down heavily on to his cold hand. His cry of Argh! was screechingly loud as was his next utterance "F**k off you time wasting "b******s!"

Making a hasty retreat to the warmth of the car I said, "That didn't go so well Andrew". "Can't win them all" he replied. "Do you think he needs a doctor?" I asked. "Put your foot down. Fancy a pint?".

Another time we visited a medium sized engineering firm near Trowbridge. The usual representatives by appointment only sign was ignored as was the norm. We had targets to meet. Being my turn to lead I approached the reception window. One of those with a glass hatch and receptionist sat behind it. I put my head to the window and stared at the girl. She stared back at me, our heads maybe two feet apart. We continued to stare at each other for some time with Andrew watching proceedings. "Well, can I help you?" she said. The window had been open all the time. That sort of got us laughing. She rang the company secretary who would see us. Up a flight of stairs and still smiling the receptionist opened the door saying "Mr Drumbottom will see you now". Inside at a huge oak desk Mr Drumbottom was peering at us. The guy was a dwarf or damn close. A real Ronnie Corbett. Well, to my eternal shame I was losing it big time. If you are out there Drumbottom, my apologies. It was the bad manners of youth and circumstance. A case of the giggles then.

I dropped my case so that I could get my head down out of sight and search for control. I failed. Andrew's lip was quivering out of control, his hands tearing into his legs for the pain to stop the smile. As Branch Manager he somehow got us through.

Back in the car, usual routine. Put your foot down. Fancy a pint?"

We always enjoyed the Bunting family's company. Andrew, Anne and their children Oliver and Amanda. Nice people. We always got on with mutual appreciation in holidays at each other's homes and watching the kids grow up.

Oliver got married to Sarah a few years ago so off we went to Belfast to have a look around the city and the wedding held at Belfast Castle a few miles outside the city. It was a civil wedding 3.00pm kick off. Around 30 friends and family waited in the foyer of the Jury Inn for the coach at 2.00pm others would be picked up first. 2.15pm came. No bus. 2.30pm. No bus. 2.45pm. No bus. A phone call to the other hotel confirmed no bus. Taxis were now called, and panic ensued. Women and children first after all Belfast had built the Titanic! Forget it. It was a scrum.

The wedding was delayed but good with a lovely reception in the Castle. Half way through proceedings and nearly two hours late, a bus came up the hill and into the car park. We found out later the driver who I will call Paddy had been early so he pulled over for 10 minutes only to fall asleep. Only in Ireland! The best Branch Trophy which Andrew and I had won at Swindon and I had won again at Newport, I gave to Oliver in memory of Andrew. Andrew would have loved that, bless him.

In the early days as a finance representative it really was a case of getting around Wiltshire seeking business. Who dares wins. Looking through my blue book recording all companies and motor dealers called on brings memories flooding back.

In September 1976 a cool 40 years ago I record, for example, doing some business with a nice young chap. Polite, well mannered and a warm smile. Clearly ambitious and solid resolve. No airs and graces. In his modest industrial unit, he had a desk and a bit of machinery. The interesting thing was to look up. A ceiling full of large rubber balls held up by netting. The idea was wheelbarrows that you could push along easily with the rubber ball.

This concept later appeared in his line of vacuum cleaners along with so many other designs and innovations. The man of course was James Dyson in those days of Kirk Dyson Designs Limited. We did some business. Who would have thought back then that he would go on destined to be one of our captains of industry? His Dyson cleaners are known worldwide and more recently his Dyson hand driers are springing up everywhere. Guess what. They are good. A hand drier that works. You don't have to finish the drying process on your shirt!

I enjoyed his Richard Dimbleby lecture on TV. Nice to see him enjoying Bath Rugby. I always want Bath to win except when they play Exeter Chiefs. Well done Sir James.

Across the county in a village called Southwick near Trowbridge another character aged around 30 ran a VW garage. Most weeks I would pop in as we did business. I ran his new car stocking finance facility and looked after any customer finance to help car sales.

The routine was to go in and without fail the grin that greeted me was warming and jovial. "Hello John. Just in time for a coffee". He was always well dressed, suit, tie and his long streaky blonde locks always prominent. Great guy, good sense of humour and excellent company. He was well known as a rallycross driver. He, at this time in 1976, was runner up in the Embassy/RAC-MSA British Rallycross and TEAC/Lydden Rallycross Championships.

The garage was ideal to sell and service VW cars but also help support his racing. He became well known in the UK for his Colorado Beetle with its striking paintwork and then his Volkswagon Golf MK1. The garage was AUTOCONTI. The man in question, step forward Mr John Button.

Jenson was born in 1980. It must have been so rewarding for John to support and be part of Jenson's brilliant Formula One career. Jenson became World Champion in 2009 and John was with him all the way. When I saw him in the pits or doing an interview, John's smile had not changed. It was my old coffee companion!

It had been a good month for Lloyds and Scottish Swindon Branch. I had arranged to finance a huge computer system, tapping into old contacts at the Westinghouse Brake and Signal Company in Chippenham. Further finance for lorries at Syms Haulage in Calne and the Fatstock Marketing Company FMC all of whom were now sought-after customers meant Swindon Branch was breaking a few records. A customary line or two copying in senior company management was my way of making sure they knew who was pulling these deals in. Well, I did not want to be a rep in Swindon for too long.

Driving back to Calne from the Swindon office, I drove through RAF Lyneham. In those days it was thriving. The Hercules airplanes were busy transporting troops and supplies all over the world. Thousands of people lived in and around the airport which made it important for the local economy. This was pre-IRA troubles. You could walk around freely looking at the planes or visiting for a Saturday disco or use the bowling alley. The RAF built the camp in 1939 and it grew into the primary Tactical Transport base for the RAF who left it in 2012. It is now used by the Ministry of Defence.

Just outside Lyneham I was drawn to a sign offering for sale a holiday chalet in Cornwall. Being in a good state and impulsively I stopped, made a few enquiries and bought it. Welcome to St Margarets Holiday Chalets in the Cornish village of Polgooth near Mevagissey. At first, all went well!

The chalet was made of wood and set with another dozen or so in a wooded valley. When the sun was out it looked pretty sat next to the old tin mine chimney. At other times it could be dark, damp and cold. We had a few holidays enjoying the area and the lovely walk down to Mevagissey and the sea. After each winter the routine was to drive down and open it up. The first job was to apply paint generously to the walls which had turned green with damp through the winter. That would be all of them. The shower room, in particular, was a sight to behold. Mr Huddy, the local plumber, would turn the water on and repair any burst pipes.

In the height of the summer it could be pleasant, so I gave it for a week as a honeymoon present to brother Gary and his bride, Jane. The idea was to save them money which could help towards a house deposit. My generous and good intentions were not necessarily appreciated. On their return Jane said she had not expected to be cold on her honeymoon! Gary said they waited in the local pub preferring the free-range chickens running everywhere to the prospect of getting back to the chalet.

Uncle Phil said it kept him fit jumping up every five minutes to put fifty pence in the electric meter! His neighbours let it a few weeks before Phil and refused to speak to them for a while. Oops. The only guy who booked it twice was a Wiltshire shepherd who thought it was home from home to his shepherd's hut. Flash turned up and said "Godwin, what the f**k have you bought here?".

Years after I sold it a local farmer who lived nearby St Margarets told me the valley was notorious for its mist, dampness and cold. REALLY!

Those Edinburgh training courses were tough. Pass and you had a good job. Fail and you were out. The training manager was a tough Scot. Role plays were common. Customer and finance man. We had a City Marine division and in a role play involving boat finance George, the manager, asked me what I knew about boats. Trying to be a wise guy I said, "Not much, but I do watch the Onedin Line on TV". It was nearly an early train.

In later years I was called up to do some of the lectures for new recruits. I now saw how tough those Ramsey Lodge managers were. One guy was singled out. "Did you see that guy with the flash red socks John? Keep an eye on him!".

Another character was our Wales and South West Regional Director, Austin Thomas, the Governor. Based in Cathedral Road, Cardiff, Austin was a bullish strong man with moustache and square shoulders. You wanted him on your side.

He took me to his club for lunch near the old Arms Park Stadium. Ladies had recently been allowed in and in his roguish way he was not happy. Tradition, heritage and standards were blemished. He ordered duck for us both, his favourite club dish. A misguided waiter said he was very sorry Mr Thomas, but the last two duck dishes had just been ordered by the ladies on another table. It was like Mount Etna erupting as Austin loudly gave a withering account of how the club was going to the dogs!

At least the men still had their own lounge and bar at his golf club. He loved the tale of a thunderstorm at the golf club. Several ladies were sheltering by the large French doors outside the men only lounge. The ladies were in disbelief as the doors slid open thinking they were to be offered refuge from the storm. Instead the old boy spoke firmly "Move along ladies please, you are blocking our view!".

Legal papers landed on Austin's desk as a result of a decision I took to safeguard the company and potentially my position. Business was flying in. A company trading near Chepstow was selling furniture at a greatly discounted price. They would take customers deposits, get them to sign for a loan on the balance from Lloyds & Scottish. Our local rep, Kevin Atkins from Bristol would pick them up and arrive in the office with maybe 20 or 30 documents. Kevin incidentally sold my Polgooth in Cornwall holiday chalet to his Dad who ran a pub in Nailsea to let to his customers. Cheers Kevin.

Anyway, the business was great but one day HOLD IT. We were paying big money to the Dealer and so was the customer. The furniture was made to order and delivered 3 to 4 months later. If the dealer went bust, disaster. I introduced a satisfaction note to be signed by the customer on receipt of the goods. Only then would we pay out. The dealer principal, a keen horse racing man, was furious at this affect on his cashflow and change of business practice. Austin was, shall we say, twitchy and sent his number 2, Derek Beard, to see me. Derek was old school. A charming gentleman he quickly concurred with me and we all stood our ground. I heard some years later that my concerns were well founded and another finance company took a hit.

Austin drove me up one of the valleys to Tredegar to visit Hills of Tredegar, one of the largest bus operators in Wales. We would see 'Foxy' Hill, the owner. Austin told me to "Listen and learn my boy". He explained its not about cost or rate it was about people, relationships and the facility. We were with 'Foxy' over an hour and Austin was in fine form. Austin talked and talked about coach finance tales over the years. 'Foxy' listened enthralled and mesmorised by this performance. Finally, as Austin drew to a close, Foxy spoke. "Wonderful Austin, now what's your rate?!".

Austin and his wife visited us in Teignmouth before his retirement. He liked our location and looking around at the views to the sea and moor he said, "You know, we all rate you John. Take your promotions and one day come back here to retire". Well, I took the promotions but kept the house and family here as well!

We played golf early one morning at Teignmouth. Jean gave Austin a line to a green using a parked car close to the 13th green. As Austin prepared, unfortunately the car moved away, and Austin's shot was fifty yards off. We laughed afterwards but not at the time!

At Newport there was a stain on the wall. A big stain right behind my manager's desk. I asked what it was and apparently one of the girls had in anger thrown a mug of tea at the previous manager. She had left and he was moved. The wall was painted and I decided to be vigilant. The world map I put up had the caption 'What else is happening today?' to keep things in perspective.

We had a meeting in my second-floor office. We heard the sound of scaffolding, which was around the building, collapsing following a metallic crushing noise. It had collapsed onto a car below. My new Ford needed a new roof!

John Parker, one of the reps, would say he was going up one of the valleys forgetting I could see the roundabout from my office as his car headed home. Elementary my dear Watson as Sherlock Holmes might say. John was a nice man. A scoutmaster. We would always double up when collecting arrears money as we did back then. Some of the area was rough. One night I drove to a farm. It was John's turn, so he got out and did the business. Walking back to the car a sheep, maybe a ram, butted John several times. I can still see John running towards the car as I, finding it hilarious, reversed away from him. He never swore. He did that night.

Our paths crossed nearly 20 years later in a different scenario. We were sat outside a hotel in the Midlands with a lake in the grounds having been given a crappy little medal for services rendered. It was a worthless piece of tack. "What are you going to do with yours John?" he asked. "Well John, to show my appreciation, I am going to skim it and see how far it gets across that lake". He was aghast as it went into the lake. About 6 skims I recall. Not bad really. John passed on too early. He was a conservationist and not wanting to waste a tree he was buried in what looked like a cardboard box. John would have laughed with us when I mentioned what we were all thinking as we walked behind it to the cemetery. Christ, I hope it doesn't bloody rain!

Richard Leigh was our area manager and keen golfer. We got on well. He liked his monthly reports on time and if results were good he let you get on with the job. He used to say I was a bit quiet at meetings but meant what I said when I spoke. Fair comment at that time. Staff appraisals were considered important. An opportunity to evaluate performance and each way dialogue to plan ahead.

My favourite annual review came in Newport. Richard had been to Cardiff Regional Office and was seeing me on his way back to Bristol.

He came into my office and said "John, I'm on the tee at 5.50 so I can't hang around. Trust me, the appraisal is very good. You've just won the best branch trophy. Never been done before at Newport. Sign here and there is your copy. I'm off."

Fair enough. A man after my own heart. Good results let's go play golf. Lovely.

An appraisal from someone else later on noted that he thought I was sensitive to criticism. What did I think?

"Well, I'm sensitive enough not to sign this trash" was my response proving he was probably right!

When working as Branch Manager in Newport my first appointment, a young and eager Nick Hunt came over from Bristol as Office Manager. He lodged with a Mrs Pattison who warmed his bed with an old brass bed pan to compensate for a general lack of heating. After sausages cooked on one side only or some other culinary disaster provided by Mrs P, Nick would sometimes turn up at our house looking for nourishment if only a plate of bread and cheese!

A feature of my management skill, and with the benefit of authority that came with being Manager, was to include a healthy sprinkling of sport into our generally hard-working week. In Newport we played a round or two at Caerleon combined with a Friday curry.   At all my posts a regular question to one of the reps would be "What are you doing this afternoon?" "Well, I've got an appointment at wherever". My response was "Right, cancel it. We are playing golf!" Or tennis. Only when targets were reached!

At Bristol where Nick joined me as a representative we had an experience we laugh at now, at the time it was painful.

After the usual routine "Cancel the appointment, we are playing tennis", we drove to the Redland Tennis Club for our regular best of three sets. In those days we were better at tennis than golf. A series of events led to an awkward situation.

Nick played a shot down the line. Stretching to get the ball I kind of twisted in the air from one direction to another. My back went and I was in agony prone on the court. Several concerned members tried to help but in that situation there is no answer other than to try and get to the changing room.   I attempted a shower, but it was hopeless. I was not capable of getting dressed. A reluctant Nick would have to help me. With little enthusiasm Nick got my pants, knelt down and had got the first foot in when, and with Nick kneeling in front of me, the changing room door opened. The member walked in and looked aghast. "Christ" he said before turning on his heels and walking straight out probably to resign and find another club, who knows? Nick did his duty and battled on before I somehow got to a chiropractor and back to Teignmouth where Anne remembers helping me crawl to bed.

A few years earlier and visiting a top chiropractor just off the Royal Crescent in Bath, an x-ray was required. The lady assistant took me to the x-ray room and told me to take my clothes off but it was fine to leave my vest on. So that is exactly what I did. She walked in the room and took one look, gave a little sound somewhere between a murmur and a sigh and hurried out. Seconds later she tapped on the door whispering through it "Oh, Mr Godwin, I meant your vest and pants!" The lesson here, be clear with instructions!

Sporting injuries can be cruel. As mentioned, my first bad back occurred playing football in Devizes. I kicked to clear a ball just as hard as I could. It hit a divot and I kicked air. The lower back went into a spasm. One of the supporters shouted, "Run it off Godwin" "Thanks for those astute medical words of wisdom" Prat! I had a weak lower back for years. It did not restrict my sport particularly, but it would play up if only once a year. Enter Lorraine Avery who was then working in a sports injuries clinic in Newton Abbot. She looked me over thoroughly and diagnosed a lateral shift and prolapsed disc. If you draw a line from your nose to your navel or belly button it should be straight. Mine was not.

Lorraine, to whom I will always be grateful, sorted me out and gave me a short pre-sport stretching routine which has served me well for years. To Lorraine, now a member at my golf club, thank you.

Let's be fair. The finance industry breeds, even attracts, people who particularly on the sales side work and play hard. It's the culture.

We had a company Golf Day at Turnberry up in South West Scotland. Gold taps and telephones in the bathrooms, top class facilities. No expense was spared. The wives were invited and pampered. We played our golf competition on the course that has hosted so many tournaments including The Open 7 times. We played the main world-famous Ailsa course.

This was the course where Tom Watson and Jack Nicklaus had fought it out in 1977. The 18th hole was renamed the 'Dual in the Sun Hole' in recognition.

Anyway, I played Joe Average and in the knowledge I would not be receiving a prize at the award ceremony, after dinner did the right and proper thing to support the company by attacking the free bar. Our table for dinner was at the back and the wine flowed nicely. The prize ceremony was almost over and the MD announced one further award. Who had played the Par Threes best. Hold it. In a dismal round generally, I was one under par for the par threes. The crystal glassware in our cabinet I view partly as a golf prize but also for a miraculous walk to the stage and back. Taking the prize from the MD and seeing two hands held out luckily I chose the correct one to shake. The word got out that the marketing manager was fired for being grossly over budget for the day.

Chapter 30

DON'T DRIVE ON THE FAIRWAY!

There was a time when I took golf seriously enough to actually practice. Over time I realised that to practice playing poor shots leaves you no better off other than some exercise and fresh air. You really need advice from your club professional. This should help providing the pro knows what he is talking about. They usually do. Years ago, a pro looked at my left-handed swing before smiling, waiting for his expert advice, I was set back when he asked, "Have you considered playing right handed?" Charming! Like any sport talent is a gift not bestowed in equal measure. Some guys have a natural gift of timing and balance. For some, golf is hard work. The handicap system helps people of all abilities play in competitions. Rightly cream usually rises to the top and the better players win especially as the course is extended to its full length with tees as far back as possible. It favours the big hitters and lower handicaps.

Anyway, seeking to make the most of my average golfing ability around thirty years ago I was hitting balls on the practice area. My Saab car was parked on the road nearby. Looking across to the eleventh tee it was clear something was wrong. A golfer was laying in front of the tee and his 3 partners were in distress. This was pre-mobile phones, so action was needed. I dived into my Saab and took the quickest route to the clubhouse for a 999 call. That happened to be straight up the course back up the 10th fairway.

Roaring into the car park the office manager waved at me to slow down. "Never mind that, we have a heart attack victim. Get your secretary to call an ambulance." He did. "Now is there a doctor around?" "Yes" he said. "Out playing. Started just over an hour ago." "Right, get in, let's go find the doctor."

Now we are bombing back down the 10th. "Keep off the fairway" he cried. Well, you normally want to be on the fairway on a golf course and anyway, this was an emergency. We found the doctor on the 7th green putting. "Quick a chap has had a heart attack" "Well, I don't know what you want me to do" came the reply. Unbelievable.

We drove to the scene and the doctor took over from Dave Bennett who was trying the kiss of life. The ambulance arrived with the electric defibrillator. Unfortunately, it was all to no avail but not a bad way to go I guess, playing golf with friends,

At this point a couple of guys asked if it would be okay for them to play through. They were quickly told to go forth and multiply. The ambulance took the body away. Dave was shook up so I put his clubs in the Saab. The other two players decided to play on and finish the round. "There is nothing we can do and he would have wanted us to finish our golf" said one of them!

I mentioned pre-mobile phones. Well, as they began to appear a mobile phone incident led to my first entry to the club suggestion book. It went like this.

I was stood on the tenth tee about to unleash my usual 250-yard arrow of a drive down the centre of the fairway. At the top of my swing a mobile phone started ringing in the bag of one of the other players. My golf ball, instead of going straight, was last seen heading off at 45 degrees towards Dawlish. A gentleman on the 18th green equally put off missed his tap in putt and was heard to say "Oh, for f***s sake!"

After thanking the mobile phone owner for his contribution to my round, I asked him to turn it off and put it away. "May I suggest that mobile phones be banned from the course and clubhouse and only be carried switched off for medical emergency."

After the Saab incident I can see that if switched off it's useful to have one. Anyway, the committee agreed and the mobiles were duly banned!

The suggestion book is useful for thought out ideas for the good of the club. It is not intended for the wise-guy who suggests a plate of chips is overpriced or the smart alec who suggests there are too many ladies on the course and that they should stick to the kitchen and bedroom. Unsigned of course!

He would have been one of those opposed to ladies having a vote in club matters. For years the ladies never got the percentage needed at the club's Annual General Meeting to give them the vote. And then it happened and they made it. Three things influenced my vote in their favour.

Tenerife, a gorgeous girl wearing only a thong has volunteered to take a photo.

Number one, we had a lady Prime Minister in Margaret Thatcher. Number two, I had two daughters and most influential of all, Molly Cayless who would later be Lady Captain when I was Club Captain jabbed me in the back. She was sat behind me and leaned forward with a jab and a clear instructional directive "Get your hand up Godwin!"

Nick Hunt, Alan Yates and I have played golf most weeks for over 25 years. The three amigos. Our annual game for the three amigo's trophy is epic. A highlight in our sporting calendar. It rates right up there alongside the Open, Wimbledon and the Cup Final for three athletes in this titanic battle of the bulge! It takes place on our home course at Teignmouth or we have ventured to Spain and Turkey a few times. These have been fun and the ladies come as well. Someone has to do the packing!

One boys only trip to France was eventful. It was three sets of clubs, cases and boys into my Nissan Terrano and onto the Plymouth Ferry. One course was closed completely flooded. We made the most of it with lunch at the chateau style clubhouse. A French omelette for three the size of a dustbin lid. Various wines. We agreed to take a drink of something different thinking cognac or such. I pointed at one bottle which looked interesting so took a drink. Raspberry cordial. Aaah!

After one game pretty boy Nick did not want to go into the clubhouse at Golf Club de L'Odet without freshening up on a hot day. His case was at the hotel so I put my hand into my toiletry bag to find a deodorant for him. Fumbling around I sliced my finger on my razor. Blood everywhere. In the clubhouse, as normal, I wanted a souvenir golf ball. The assistant in the pro shop, rather than sell me the standard ball with the club name on, made a phone call. A few minutes later a well-dressed lady

3 Amigos cooling off in Turkey

Three Amigo's, Spain

appeared introducing herself as Madam President de la Club L'Odet. She walked me to her office before opening a safe. She gave me a rather nice golf ball with club name and logo on it. The price should have included a few club shares but how could I refuse. It sits with other 'specials' in my dining room.

We stayed in a small town on the coast. Very pretty with local fish produce. The problem being out of season was that basically, in the evenings, it was shut. Walking around one night searching for somewhere to eat we heard music coming from a café up a side street. We marched in to the Rolling Stones blasting out 'It's only rock and roll, but I like it'. Never mind food, it was local lager time. The locals were smoking and the smell took me back to the Caribbean if you get my drift or should I say spliff.

I still have nightmares about that return ferry crossing. Who sets off in a force eight gale when other ferries are cancelling. Getting into Plymouth and off the ferry was beyond relief. It was a quick drive up to the Devon Causeway and into the sanctuary of a pub to reflect on the trip and have a home coming pint.

By the way, the 3 amigos have a sense of humour. The 3 of us were in the rough when the head green keeper drove past in his buggy only stopping with a grin to say, "Feel free to use the fairway gentlemen!" Thank you, Justin and keep up the good work.

Another trip to Spain to play at Valle Del Este was interesting. We went to Desert Springs for a round. Ian Botham has a villa there. The golf was slightly strange as some holes have a fairly narrow fairway built especially and grassed for golf. Either side its all great expanses of desert sands. The place could have been used to film Lawrence of Arabia. Anyway, it's still a good course with some nice features. The problem came when Nick's knee collapsed. One more attempt at a shot which shanked into some

Six Amigo's

German players on the adjoining hole. We know they were German because with Nick now hobbling badly, they refused to drive him in their buggy. We were not happy with their attitude and tension built as we started whistling the Dambusters theme.

Anyway, that was Nick's golf well and truly gefickt to stay with the German theme. He was gefickt off. He also thought these Germans were a bunch of gefickters while he normally speaks highly of them. We got him back to the pool where, stuck with his predicament, he proceeded to get Brahms and Liszt or besoffen, sitting around with our ladies was like appearing on TV in Loose Women he later reported.

Our flight home did not start well at the airport. The tannoy system bleeped. The announcer asked for Mr N Hunt to go to security after we had dropped our suitcases. He quickly came back with a grin saying it was my case they were interested in. He had grassed me up!

Reporting to security I was promptly arrested and taken by two armed policemen to a small room. A tour guide came to interpret. It seems that I had a gun in my case and the x-ray machine proved it. This was serious. Had someone interfered with the case?

And then it came to me. I had bought Grandson Jensen a toy cowboy gun complete with holster. I laughed and made to open the case. Big mistake. Out came a truncheon and real gun. The second policeman was now fumbling in the case. Anne's knickers were flying around and finally he found the toy gun. He sort of laughed at my explanation and allowed us to travel complete with the present.

And the good news? The security works. Happy travelling.

TEIGNMOUTH
GOLF CLUB

Chapter 31

TEIGNMOUTH GOLF CLUB

If you drive towards Teignmouth on the Exeter Road, you will be aware of the pretty woods and moorland. Passing through Little Haldon stop your car on the plateau just before the road starts to drop down into Teignmouth or the gem of South Devon as it is sometimes called. You can admire the view over towards Exmouth and beyond. Walk around this plateau and you can see on a clear day as far as Portland Bill. You can see Tors up on Dartmoor. You can look down from your 800 feet vantage point to Teignmouth and Shaldon. Up the Teign Estuary to Newton Abbot. Around the coast to Torbay. You will also almost certainly be trespassing. To fully enjoy the best views of the above you will need to be on Teignmouth Golf Course. Visitors welcome I hasten to add. It's a friendly club!

The air is wonderful and fresh straight off the sea. A good night's sleep is normally guaranteed after a round of golf. You feel good. If only the air could be bottled! Funnily enough, and believe it or not, bottled air is available in Beijing as we witnessed a few years ago. Most people wear mask filters to combat the smog. How lucky are we then?

The club was formed in 1924. Tom Scott, the Editor of Golf Illustrated, once wrote that he knew of few golf courses throughout the length and breadth of the country which have as splendid a situation as the Teignmouth Club in South Devon. Exactly.

As the stone at the club entrance displays, the course was designed by the world-famous architect Dr Alister MacKenzie also designer of Augusta National USA.

Augusta of course is in Georgia and home of the Masters. He designed courses all around the world including Royal Melbourne in Australia and Cypress Point in the USA. St Charles Country Club in Canada and Lahinch Golf Club in Ireland. He was a doctor with the British Army in the Boer War. During World War I he made significant contributions to military camouflage which he saw as closely related to golf club design. He was based in America towards the end of his life and died in Santa Cruz California two months before the first Masters tournament. He is a member of the World Cup Hall of Fame. Sadly, he is reputed to have died in poverty. Writing in a letter to Augusta he wrote

"Can you possibly let me have at any rate five hundred dollars to keep us out of the poor house? I have been reduced to playing golf with four clubs. I am at the end of my tether. No-one has paid me a cent since last June. We have mortgaged everything we have and have not yet been able to pay the nursing expenses of my wife's operation."

A divorce from his first wife and an expensive lifestyle in California had caught up and not getting paid on time meant he was insolvent. A great golf club designer but maybe not so good with financial management.

MacKenzie, when a doctor, advised patients to take up golf for their health. He felt that a good golf course should provide a stern test for a good player but not prove impossible for average players. A variety of shots should be needed. Undulation without big hills. His trademark two-tier greens are featured at Teignmouth along with a nice mix of length. We have six par threes, three par fives and nine par fours. That's

off the longer white tees. It can vary and off yellow tees the par 4's increase to five. The ladies red tees equate to the men's yellow tees except on holes 15 and 18 where due to length they get an extra shot. That's easy then. Now just go and hit the ball!

Each hole has a name. The names were arrived at after members were asked for suggestions.

1.	Bishops Palace.	Beyond the green lie the ruins at Bishopsteignton.
2.	Sandy Parlour.	Bucket and spade may be required.
3.	Mapping Stone.	It's in the name folks. The stone is left of the fairway.
4.	MacKenzie.	Course designer.
5.	Gypsy Corner.	Clue in the name. None around now.
6.	Humber Down.	Nearby location.
7.	Three Tors.	Look right of the fairway and see them on Dartmoor.
8.	The Road Hole.	A road runs to the side of the hole. Careful driving!
9.	Dymonds Way.	Mr Dymond was club pro for over 40 years.
10.	Portland.	Can be seen 40 miles away over the sea if clear.
11.	Vardons Mount.	Harry Vardon Golfer.
12.	Harold's Folly.	Easy to hit the road here.
13.	Siberia.	Furthest hole from the clubhouse. Can be cold!
14.	Little Haldon.	Location.
15.	Holcombe Top.	Holcombe Village is a couple of miles downhill.
16.	Hells Mouth.	Tricky par 3.
17.	Dip.	Dog leg downhill.
18.	Last Quarry.	Drive over the last quarry.

On the first hole you can still see an observation tower put up in the Second World War 1939-45. The air ministry took over and flattened the 13th and 14th holes to make a landing strip. Hundreds of posts were strategically placed on fairways to stop any enemy aircraft landing. Another bit of history going further back concerns the 9th fairway which is home to an old burial ground. Mr Dymond mentioned this in his video of the club's history which no-one seems to know where it is. Such a shame. Search party required.

The 18-hole course effectively has two 9-hole loops meaning we have the advantage of two starting points. The course is a fair test of golf. You do not want to get in the heather. Its tough to get out if you find your ball! In the summer a gentle breeze will cool you on a hot day. In the winter, of course, it can be exposed to the elements. Getting older, my clubs seem to spend longer in the garage than they used to at times of bad weather. We also now have buggies which, while defeating the object of a good walk for exercise, can help a member or guest who might otherwise struggle to play at all.

I became a member in 1984. 35 years on the course so far. It's been good. A key part of my sporting and social scene. If you have not played at Teignmouth treat yourself. If you don't play golf, then come and say hello anyway. It's worth it for the panoramic views and the fresh air.

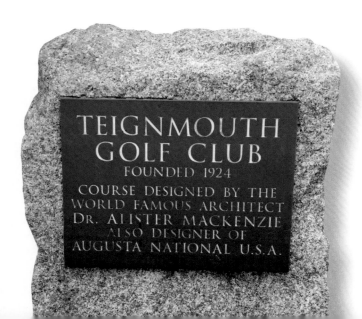

Teignmouth Golf Club

A GREAT PLACE FOR A WEDDING

Teignmouth Golf Club

A GREAT PLACE FOR A FANCY DRESS PARTY

An invitation to
Anne & John's Joint 50th Party
on SATURDAY, 7th SEPTEMBER, 2002
at TEIGNMOUTH GOLF CLUB from 7.30 p.m.
You are encouraged to come in

Fancy Dress
BUT WE / WELCOME YOU ANYWAY!

R.S.V.P.: Annie Oakley (Godwin) or Jesse James   Tel: (01626) 770447
24 ST. MARYS ROAD, TEIGNMOUTH, DEVON. TQ14 9LY

Tony Hodgeson

Chapter 32

GOLF CLUB CAPTAIN

The telephone rang at home one Sunday evening. "Hello Godders, it's Tim Foggarty here" he said in his distinctive and friendly voice. Interesting. I knew Tim as we were both long standing members of Teignmouth Golf Club. "You will know I am to be Captain next year. I would like you to be my Vice-Captain and then of course Captain the following year. No rush, give it some thought and let me know. Ring me back in the next 10 minutes!".

Relax it's only a cup match at Sidmouth

Club Team Squad

Tim is a larger than life character. Life and soul of the party. Plenty to say about everything usually in a humorous and entertaining way. And now he was proving to also be a good judge of character in his decision making!! We had got to know each other on the course and at various club functions. On one occasion we had shared a taxi with a couple of other boys. Such was the banter after a merry evening spent mainly at the bar that we drove past my house without really noticing. Arriving at Tim's it was all in for a brandy or two. I ended up walking home that night!

On another occasion Tim was present for my little victory speech having won the annual Captain's Day Golf competition. At the presentation, and having thanked the ground staff for the state of the course, my playing partners and the Captain I announced how pleased I was to win and get my name on the Honours Board in what was my last game of golf at Teignmouth Golf Club (silence in the room) as an amateur!! That went down well and got a good laugh.

Tim obviously liked what he saw and logged it!

I realised the invitation to be Club Captain was to be for a rather special year. It would run from the end of February 1999 through to February 2000 and would therefore include the celebrations of the club's 75th Anniversary and, of course, the Millenium. Time for a little thought and decision making.

Having been invited did I want to do it? First instinct was YES, an honour to be proud of. Could I do it and contribute to the club and members? YES. I had done a certain amount of public speaking over the years mainly in the finance industry at meetings and conferences. I had been involved in teams and understood the need for organization and club traditions and standards. Could I afford it? Well, it would

Captains Day

cost me a few bob but that went with the territory so, YES. Could I afford the time? YES. I was still working but golf was now my main hobby. I am not a DIY man or gardener! My children were older now. Would my family support me over the two years Vice-Captain then Captain? YES.

Anne over the years has always been supportive of my love for sport whether it was football, tennis, rugby or golf. She has always encouraged me to keep playing and be fit and active. As an outgoing and warm person, she mixes well in company, a good Captain's wife. She would need to brush up a little on terminology. When caddying she had a habit of asking "What stick to you want next?!"

Was my golf good enough? Yes, just about. You did not need to be the club champion. I was Joe Average. Around 16 handicap at the time. I was competitive and had won the Captain's Day Competition twice, the Summer Fourball twice, the Winter Foursome and the mixed Scown Cup and Rosebowl. Also, I had won the Cock of the Course competition played through the winter months. In doubles team selection is important. My appreciation to Messrs Higgins, Armitage, Hubbard and Ansell. I was never short on confidence and hopefully mixed well.

A Captain is at the helm for one year only. Delegation is important, and you need good people around you. The Captain is a figure head. A custodian of the club's heritage carrying the baton for the year. Ok. Decision made. I rang Tim back the same evening "Count me in Tim, you have my full support."

The year as Vice-Captain is useful. You help the Captain where you can. You run the South Devon League team, get in the swing of the Board and Social meetings. The Greens Committee. You look, listen, and plan your own approach. You identify

Captains Drive in 1999

who you think can help you. Who do you not want involved. Members are aware you are Captain elect. One or two might even buy you a drink and hint they would like to follow you. It falls to the Captain to select his successor. There is also a list of "possible" which past Captains chew over. The odd black ball can rule a name out. The man selected is then rubber stamped by the Board. Things run along quickly as Vice-Captain and before you know it, it's your turn for the big job. The AGM. Your new red blazer, a little speech. Next morning CAPTAIN'S DRIVE IN!

Hanging in the club house is an old wooden driver. Traditionally it comes down once a year. The new Captain complete with a good audience of members, friends and family gather at the club the day after the Annual General Meeting. It is a pleasant occasion. Drinks, reception and the Captain's Drive in. A single drive off the first tee to cement the new Captain's year in office. Members buy £1 tickets to guess how far the drive will go. The winner gets half the money, the rest goes to the Captain's charity. At an appropriate time everyone goes to the first tee and, with the local press in attendance, he drives off. The drive is measured with great care. The Captain's length is measured so to speak. It is of course a daunting but not to be taken too seriously occasion. Having said that, an air shot, hook or shank is not desirable given the audience together with the local press. A picture in the paper with a caption 'New Captain misses the ball, what a plonker!' or 'New Captain shanks towards the sea' is not what you want really.

All routine. Except for one thing. Hold it. The driver is a normal right-handed club. Now I play left handed. What to do? Option one was to enter into the spirit of things.

2000 Captains Charity Day team winners, Hubbard, Godwin and Fell

Have a go right handed and so what if the ball only went 50 yards. Option two, break with tradition and use a left-handed club. I went for option one. For the record 117 yards. Honour and tradition preserved. Time for a drink and to say a few words in which I introduced my family, wife, daughters and mother. This went down well and I was pleased to see it repeated the following year. A nice touch of togetherness.

The choice of Captain's charity is personal. I went for the NSPCC because any form of cruelty or suffering where children are concerned is abhorrent. 75% went to the NSPCC. 25% went to our local girl guides. Anne has been treasurer to the friends of guiding for over 25 years so I knew they always struggle. A cash boost for a local good cause seemed a good idea. During the year, events are held to raise money the highlight being the Captain's Charity Day when you hope for good weather. We were lucky to get a glorious sunny day. Given the alfresco refreshments halfway round, it helps. Who wants a soggy burger?

These events bring out the best in people. Volunteers to help with score cards, starters, ball spotters, on some holes to keep play moving. Refreshment helpers, raffle ticket sellers. The Captain and his lady greet everyone and it's an enjoyable day. It ends with a prize giving and auction of donated items from supporting businesses, local traders and other golf clubs putting up say a round for four. One guy turned up forgetting the course was closed for Captain's Day. He wanted to play but refused to pay or even make a donation. Unbelievable given he is a multi-milllionaire. He left in a huff after being told where to go by our intrepid starter. It takes all sorts. 99% lovely. It's the other 1%! One guy not even a playing member was renowned for

Past Captains and Presidents Dinner 1999

moaning about everything and everyone. In one of the less agreeable of duties I had a little word with him asking if he might be more comfortable and perhaps he should look for another club. It had the desired effect. He stayed and was even heard to be complimentary.

A few weeks into the Captain's tenure he hosts the formal Past Captains and Presidents black tie dinner. A nice meal. Port and brandy. The table is set according to the year you were Captain or President. Oldest one end down to the new Captain at the head of the table. As the years go on of course you find yourself sliding down the table.

The conveyer belt that is life of course keeps on moving along just like the words from the song Old Man River. You know the one. Usually circa 20 attend. After the meal before a customary joke from everyone I said a few words. One of my better evenings. Mobile phones were now in fashion. I had a spoof mobile in my pocket which I set off as a prop a couple of times. No-one knew it was not for real. It went something like this.

"Gentlemen, it is a great honour to be here tonight as the new Captain of Teignmouth Golf Club (mobile rings). Excuse me please gentlemen.

"Hello darling, I can't really talk now but yes, it was wonderful for me too"

"Yes, I liked your nipple studs"

"Look I can't really talk"

Prize giving evening for winners

"Well, yes, your husband is here. Do you want to speak to him?"

"Sorry about that chaps. This is a wonderful club and (mobile rings)

"Hello Norman" (very well known and liked Club stalwart. Never Captain or President).

"I can't talk now. I am speaking at the Past Captains and Presidents Dinner. What do you mean, why were you not invited. Because you have not been Captain or President."

"So what? So that is the reason Norman. It is a fundamental requisite that to be invited to the past Captains and Presidents dinner you have actually had to be a past Captain or President".

It all seemed to go well. One previous Captain who had founded the dinner many years ago took the trouble to contact me and thank me for bringing something to the dinner which he felt gave it rejuvenation and how much he had enjoyed it. Praise indeed coming from Frank Hiles later President of the Devon Golf Union. A top man. I appreciated his kind words.

I tried to be around and to support the various sections with circa 700 members there is usually something going on. The Seniors were good fun. Their Captain, Derek Nazer, and I got on very well. He enjoyed a drop of scotch as much as I do. We visited each other's home for a drink or three and he was very respectful that while he was Captain of the Senior Section there was only one Club Captain. In some years that is not always so evident! I was asked to present prizes at the Seniors Annual piss

Captain and Lady Captain

up which masquerades as a presentation dinner. These boys know how to prove that boys will be boys regardless of age. It was announced that on reaching 80 as per tradition member x no longer needed to pay his £5 Seniors subscription. He thanked the Seniors Captain and suggested the subscription should be increased to £10!

I was lucky with the ladies so to speak. Their Captain, Molly Cayless, is a friend and we were on the same wavelength. We got on wonderfully. I made a point of turning up wearing my red Captain's blazer to support the ladies' team at one or two matches. Her diary was busier than mine! One of the waitresses had a baby. Molly and I were pictured holding the baby in the dining room. A photograph soon appeared with a caption reading Club and Lady Captain bonding well.

We re-opened the 16th green together, the idea was we would find the green on the short part three. Club professional, Peter Ward, did a video to be shown in the clubhouse. Molly hit the green first time. I took a number of shots before hitting the centre of the green. Peter was kind enough to edit the video. He removed some shots and apparently some rather choice language. Thank you, Peter.

Molly and her husband Paul are good company. Paul was later to become Club Captain himself and did a very good job. Both are part of the fabric of the club. Funny now to watch our grandsons play in the same football team. It's in the genes! Jensen and Alfie are good players. It's great to see them playing sport rather than playing on a laptop!

Man of the match

Club Stalwart Dave Turner 'Mr Reliable'

Jeff Boyne always good for a laugh

Juniors future winners

Mr. James H Armstrong
General Manager
Augusta National Golf Club
Augusta   P.O.Box 2086
Georgia 30903 U S A

27th August 1998

Dear Mr Armstrong,

Teignmouth Golf Club, is located in Devon, which is in the South of England. It is a
Golf Club with outstanding coastal and moorland views, amongst the best in the
United Kingdom. Teignmouth Golf Club was founded in 1924 and next year we
celebrate our 75th Anniversary and of course this leads on to the Millennium
celebrations.   Also, I am honoured to have been asked to be Club Captain during that
period.

Our Golf Course was designed by Dr. Alister Mackenzie, and I enclose a photograph
of the stone which acknowledges our link with Augusta National. I am writing to you
to see if it would be possible to bring a team of say 12 golfers to play at Augusta
National, preferably against 12 of your members, e.g. over two rounds of golf. This
would be a great honour for us and a unique part of our celebrations. October or
November for example in 1999, would be a good time but we are open minded on that.

The Anglo American link is a strong one and long may it continue. I look forward to
your thoughts and I shall be obliged if you will kindly reply in confidence to me
personally at the following address;- "Valhalla", 24 St Marys Road, Teignmouth,
Devon, England TQ14 9LY.

My very best regards from England.

Yours sincerely

John Godwin
Vice Captain ,Teignmouth Golf Club

Chapter 33

AUGUSTA OR WOODBURY

The Annual Captain's Safari basically is an away day to another usually local golf course for the men who want to play. I wanted mine to be special so, bearing in mind our mutual course designer, Alister MacKenzie, my thinking was to go to Augusta, home of the Masters in Georgia, USA. My letter to the General Manager, James H Armstrong Junior, follows and then his response which was posted up onto the club noticeboard for all members to share.

I have a soft spot for Woodbury. Playing with my nephew I had a hole in one on the 18th hole. A 7 iron over the lake. Two bounces and in, right in front of the clubhouse and a round of applause on the walk to the green. Magic. Funnily enough, my other hole in one was at the North Wilts Golf Club with George's Dad, my brother Gary. That came on the par 3 third. A poor shot short of the green that somehow ran onto the green and into the hole. A fluke but I'll take it.

Holes in one for me at Teignmouth after 35 years to date. None!!

So, we had a good day out at Nigel Mansell's Woodbury Park and not Augusta. Look at the money we saved. So much for the Anglo-American special relationship. Not so special for our friends at Augusta it seems.

Our Club Secretary, Derek Holloway, retired during my year. A good golfer he plays now with the Seniors and it is always good to see him around the club and town. His daughter Vicky became County Champion. When Derek left I was able, at his

ROBERT TYRE JONES, JR.
President in Perpetuity

CLIFFORD ROBERTS
Chairman in Memoriam

JACKSON T. STEPHENS
Chairman Emeritus

WILLIAM W. JOHNSON
Chairman

Augusta
National
Golf
Club

September 23, 1998

Mr. John Godwin
"Valhalla"
24 St. Marys Road
Teignmouth, Devon
England TQ14 9LY

Dear Mr. Godwin:

Congratulations on the 75th Anniversary of Teignmouth Golf Club. I regret to advise you that the only way playing privileges can be arranged is by a member. Also note, that the member must accompany his guests on the Club grounds. Club custom does not permit the staff to approach members regarding the sponsorship of individuals on the golf course as you must be acquainted with a member and be personally invited by him.

I am sure that you will understand why this Club found it necessary to rule out the issuance of guest cards when I explain that we receive thousands of requests for these privileges -- far more than any private club could undertake to accommodate.

Sincerely,

James H. Armstrong, Jr.
General Manager

CLUB SAFARI

:dj

O.K. SO WE ARE NOT GOING TO AUGUSTA!
HOWEVER WE WILL BE GOING TO WOODBURY PARK
PLEASE PUT JUNE 23 IN YOUR DIARY/
LIST AND DETAILS LATER.

John G.

TEIGNMOUTH GOLF CLUB LIMITED

MENS SAFARI

on WED. 23rd JUNE, 1999 at

ITINERARY

MEET AT WOODBURY AT 9.30 am

Coffee on arrival

9 holes on the Acorns course - Tee times from 10.00 am

Sandwich Lunch

18 holes on the Oaks Championship course
- Tee times from 1.00 pm

2 Course Roast Dinner

£47.00 per person - To include all the above & prizes

WOODBURY PARK REQUIRE PAYMENT OF £47.00 PER PERSON
ONE WEEK IN ADVANCE, THEREFORE THE FEES MUST BE PAID
TO OUR SECRETARY BY SUNDAY, 13th JUNE

PLEASE INSERT NAMES ON THE LIST PROVIDED

leaving do, to thank him for his service. I recounted a true story told to me by Mike Jarret. Many years before Mike had visited a number of local clubs with a view to joining. Teignmouth was not his closest club but Derek made him feel so welcome that he joined. The beautiful golf course helped but Derek had that ability to connect with people.

Derek played a lot of golf himself and it was known he was often on the course, the Club President, Derek Hair, followed me with a few words of his own and brought the house down when he said, "I want to thank Derek and to wish him a long and happy retirement. To be perfectly honest, I thought he had already retired."

The Juniors were coming along. Tony Hodgson took on the running of the Junior Section. A previous Captain himself, he did a brilliant job ensuring a talented group understood discipline. Dress smartly, be punctual, practice. Under Tony our fine crop of youngsters flourished and remarkably became English and then United Kingdom Junior Champions in 2003. Boys to be proud of. Included in the team were Jon Axford, now Assistant Pro at Teignmouth, and a good coach. We call him 'the guru', font of all knowledge, ever popular who works well with our Club Professional the one and only Rob Selley. Also in the team Luke Radford, later to be Club Champion.

When one lad went on to play for Devon it was my pleasure to sort out some new irons for him. Any outstanding young talent should be encouraged. Chris Durham, Nick Osborne , Jason Gallagher and Lloyd Gardner played. Hits the ball a mile. Well done boys and well managed Tony. As an ex-Naval Officer Tony was the man for the job. A good competitor, Tony and I have had some single knock out matches over the years with honours even. He is a no-nonsense character.

The year went well and smoothly. Sean Mason, son of Keith, became Club Champion. The Masons are all keen golfers and competitive. Jean was Ladies Champion many times and had a hole in one two days running. About to drive on the twelfth I witnessed her second hole in one on the adjoining 16th. Keith was always good company on tour and enjoyed loosening straps and watching bags fall off buggies as they pulled away!

I got up early and spent a morning with the green staff just to get the feel of what they did. First priority was to get the kettle on before venturing out to do what they do! Our course these days is in great shape. My only concern is that MacKenzie kind of knew what he was doing. Don't tinker too much boys!

We had a Chairman in Brian Eastwood for a few dollars more let me tell you the good, the bad and the ugly of his role. As a retired Police Personnel Officer, he was most capable. Just what you need at the helm. Staff matters, policy, meetings of the board etc. Brian was on the ball. The Captain needs to just get on and does not have time for example to deal with an occasional member of staff who gets above his or her station or is not pulling in the right direction.

The members were great. With any cross section of people you get all sorts but in the main we have a good mix and a healthy, friendly club with good competitive golf and some outstanding players.

T.G.C. NEWS

Teignmouth Golf Club Ltd

CAPTAINS MILLENNIUM MESSAGE

January 2000

Volume 1, Issue 5

May I take this opportunity to extend Seasonal Greetings to all members of the Club. My very best wishes to you all for the year 2000.

1999 has been a busy year at Teignmouth Golf Club. We have enjoyed the Club's 75th Anniversary celebrations and had a total eclipse thrown in for good measure.

On the course our competitions as always have been competitive and the course has been generally in good order. The Ladies have carried all before them on the county scene while the Men have come close and can progress. The Junior Section is growing and the Seniors continue to enjoy themselves.

I would like to thank the Seniors Section for presenting to the Club new table mats and coasters which will soon be on display in the Club's restaurant.

On the personnel front we have a new catering team and a new Club Manager. The Millennium Ball is approaching at the time of writing this and thanks go to David & Jo Wright and Bernie & Pam Morris in particular for their sterling work in organising the event.

As Club Captain may I thank you for your support during the year. May I also draw your attention to the work, time and effort put in by the Officers and various Committee members for the benefit of us all. Well done to them and thank you from us all.

Finally we may be entering a new Millennium but somethings will not change. We still have our wonderful course to play, views to enjoy and friends to greet at the 19th! Long may they continue.

Good Golfing and Enjoyment at Teignmouth Golf Club.

John Godwin

Club Captain

Apology from Club Manager

Please Note:- Last months item regarding the new Vice Captain should have read, The Vice Captain Malcolm Tester proposed Ian Butterfield as his new Vice Captain this was endorsed by the Board. Malcolm also requested that a meeting between himself and Past Captain's was held to help him decide which members should, or should not, be considered for this important position. I apologise for any misunderstanding this may have caused.

Club Manager Steve Wright

Special points of interest:

- Captain's Message
- From the archives 1925 (ladies)
- Pat Goodey New Lady Captain
- Seniors Turkey Trot Great Success
- Fixtures for the 2000 part one
- Re-planting heather
- Apology to Vice Captain

Chapter 34

THREE BALLS

The 75th Anniversary Ball was a black tie and gown occasion. It was a sell out as was the Millennium Ball held on 31st December 1999. 7 for 7.30pm with music until 2.30am. Party time! Such was the demand for tickets that we hired a marquee extension to allow for more members and friends to enjoy seeing us into 2000 and a new millennium. As Captain, I said a few words but kept it brief at both balls which makes sense when people are enjoying drinks, fine dining and entertainment. It was quite eerie on the stroke of midnight. I went out to the first tee and drove a ball, the first ball to be hit at Teignmouth Golf Club this new millennium. Just seemed a nice thing to do for posterity.

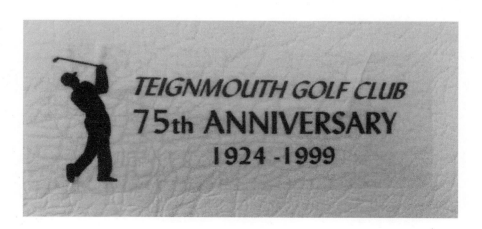

The traditional Captain's Ball was the third in the trilogy of big Balls to organize if you pardon the expression. Tradition dictated booking a hotel such as the Royal in Torquay, but I was cautious. We had already had two balls. How far would members support and pockets stretch? I decided to play safe. The Captain's Dinner would be held in our own clubhouse. Income for the club, no away travelling or overnight stay and less pressure on numbers to worry about. But I needed a trump card. What resulted was a sell out and one of the best nights ever held at the club, members opinion not just mine. I arranged for the dance band of the Royal Marines to entertain us and provide the music. Tickets were red hot and so were the Royal Marines. Security was high in those days with the IRA threat and their bus guarded throughout. It was a classic night.

Being my Captain's Ball, a longer speech was required. It went like this.

"Mr President, Mr Chairman, Distinguished Guests from other clubs and the County, Fellow Athletes and members of the Temperance Society, Ladies and Gentlemen welcome to the Teignmouth Golf Club Annual Ball.

I will not be too long as we have some serious drinking to do tonight.

Just one apology this evening from my Summer Doubles partner Richard Armitage. "Godders, have a great night. Would love to be with you but I am rather restricted at night under the terms of my Community Service Order". (Only joking!).

There was also a message left earlier for my old mate Adrian Whittle from the Manager at Burtons. He would like his hire suit back as early as possible as it is needed again for tomorrow night.

We are fortunate to be entertained tonight by the Dance Band of the Royal Marines. Like some of our members, their reputation goes before them. My family has military tradition. My Grandfather was an extra in the film Zulu. And as Michael Caine, who appeared in that film, might say, "Not many people know that!".

As a young man, I had ambitions to join the Royal Marines. May I share with you the letter they sent.

It has been a busy year with the club 75th Anniversary and the Millennium. Once again, my sincere thank you to everyone who has contributed and supported. At the start of the year one member did say to me congratulations on being Captain. It will be busy and even harder for you of course as you are not much of a golfer! Charming but true.

Our professional, Peter Ward, does not fool me. At lessons when he keeps saying "Keep your head down" I know it's because he is stood behind me laughing. I asked if I was good enough to play in our Club Palairet Team only to be advised to move to Tibet where they believe in reincarnation.

Good luck to Malcolm Tester who takes over this weekend. Malcolm, enjoy yourself. You have our full support. Now a word to the living dead.

I am pleased to see the Seniors well represented and so well led by my drinking partner Derek Nazer. We have a tradition of being last to leave the bar and it is at the bar that we do have a problem which is that the new honours board above the bar should have been put below it so that as you slide down it towards the carpet you have something to read! I did say to Derek that on finishing now as Captain we could use the next year to dry out. His reply was ahnooze dblewhicky which loosely interpreted means, don't be silly have another scotch.

May I thank Anne for her support. She has developed into a first-class caddy and no longer asks "Which stick do you want next?" Playing at St Andrews 3 weeks ago and thinking of Nick Faldo and his caddy Fanny Sunesson she said "Don't call me Annie from now on, call me Fanny or I think that's what she said. We have flowers for you Anne and thank you. I don't know where I would be without you. Well actually I do. I would be in a nightclub in Torquay most nights before going to the casino. Never mind!

Let's make this a night to remember. Please enjoy your evening. Thank you for your support and may I propose a toast which is The Guests!

One of the guests responded briefly opening with "Nice speech John, I thought you were going to call me through for a minute!".

Chapter 35

BRITISH OPEN – THERE'S A CAT IN THE CASE

"Would you like a whisky, boys?" Well, that would be a yes please and thank you then. A full English with bacon, eggs, sausage, mushrooms and tomato for breakfast and would you like a whisky boys in the evenings. Were Flash and I in heaven? Well, now. It's July 1982 and we have driven up to Troon in Scotland for the Open Golf Championship. We are staying in a town centre little bed and breakfast. The landlady, who only has three bedrooms, apologises that there is nothing in Troon. We reassure her that with a comfortable room, full English breakfast, whisky at night and the Open Golf Championship and a few local pubs we are more than happy.

On the Saturday night she asks us what we are going to do. Well, we were going to frequent a couple of pubs. "No boys, you're coming out with me". Interesting. And so, it came to pass that we put our faith and our Saturday night in the hands of our landlady. Thus far we had no reason to doubt her judgment. She was a jovial, happy go lucky widow. A good 30 years older than us. Hoping we were not going to a whist drive or domino club we set off. We ended up in Troon Town Hall. It was Big Band night. Packed and sensational. A Big Band of circa 20 band members sitting in little rows à la Glen Miller and his band. I've had better nights, but I don't remember when. Atmosphere, drinks, music. Who would have thought it? Bonus.

Back to the B & B, "You'll just be wanting a night cap boys". We caught the end of the BBC Open coverage. Arnold Palmer was being interviewed by, I think, Harry Carpenter. "Oh, that's you!" shrieked our well-oiled landlady, and it was. I had walked up to the interview and kind of stood behind and between Messrs Palmer and Carpenter. Flash observed "What a prat" perfectly reasonably but there it was on BBC. On our return brother Gary confirmed the sighting. "Thought you were going to jump on Arnold's back there for a minute"!

It was a good few days. The private planes were in and out of Prestwick Airport near the course. The golf was great. You marvel at the standard. It's a different game to the one you and I play. The recovery shots, the numbers of long putts that drop effortlessly into the hole. The vast galleries. And at the end of it all the champion. This year well it was one of the Open greats. Five times winner Tom Watson. This was number four. He was to win again in 1983. What a legend. An 8 times major winner. One of the golfing greats.

It was a near 1000-mile round trip to Troon on Scotland's West Coast. Sometimes this type of pilgrimage just has to be done if you want to be there for the experience. You have to go there and then get off the bus!

With that in mind two years later it's 1984. The Open is at St Andrews, the home of golf. Flash and I are driving up and I have brought brother Gary along for the ride.

We are looking forward to the Old Course. I played it many years later and the course has so many subtle twists and turns. It can be very weather dependent. The winds can turn it into a much more difficult proposition but then this would apply to most courses. To stand in the 17th road hole bunker is something else and I've got the photograph to prove it!

On the first night we booked into our bed and breakfast a few miles outside St Andrews. Accommodation is at a premium. We were lucky to get a room with 3 single beds and set out to get a meal in what was a small village. The local pub obliged, and we were to be up early for the golf so it was back to the room. The door was ajar and hold it! Before turning the light on we could see two bright shining eyes looking at us. We turned the light on and hold it. There is a cat in the case. Well Gary's case actually. The cat ran out of the room. Hold it again. What's that smell? The cat has crept into the case and crapped. Not content with that it has flooded the case. Gary now has a case full of cat. He had not unpacked. What to do? Well in my mind, perhaps slightly warped, I was in hysterics. Flash on the other hand was action man. Before you could say well 'Flash' he had raised the landlady and the washing machine was on. By breakfast the clothes were washed and ironed. Well played Flash!

The 1984 Open Championship was special. It was remarkable for us in so many ways. We stood by a bunker and watched Jack Nicklaus play a wonder recovery shot. The following day he played again, and the ball stayed in the bunker. He was human after all. The World's greatest golfer.

Bobby Clampett, the American golfer, was leader for a time but managed to hit one shot into the temporary stand. It ended up thirty feet beneath where we sat under the stand. Looking down I told Flash I was going under the stand to get it for a souvenir. The problem was going to be where to find it once underneath. We had a plan. Flash would squeeze our umbrella down between the steps. I would see it and know where the ball was. Directly under the umbrella. It worked, and on returning home I had the ball mounted. 'The Umbrella Trophy' for annual competition between Flash and I was born. Flash held it for a number of years mainly because after a lucky win he moved to America.

That was drastic action just to keep his hands on the Umbrella Trophy. Anyway, now he has returned I have it back! If Flash has a talent it is in food preparation. The hamper he made for the day we spent on the road hole 17th was fantastic. People came over just to look at it! Fine dining at the Open. The thing about St Andrews is that everyone from all around the World wants to visit, feel it and, if possible, play it. A wonderful centre of the golfing universe.

We were stood behind Seve Ballesteros as he shaped up to play a shot. We had encroached further than we realised. The great man turned towards us and smiled before reaching out and placing his iron club gently onto Gary's nose.

"Maybe you are a little too close, yes?" he said. Seve went on to win the tournament. 1984 Open Champion at the home of golf!

Chapter 36

ANYONE FOR TENNIS?

What a wonderful game. I had always enjoyed tennis. Especially when brother Gary and I played our cousins James and Daniel Slade for the family bragging rights. It's a game of grace, speed and timing or at least it should be.

It took on added dimension when we moved to Newport. A few hundred yards from our house was the Stow Park Lawn Tennis Club. Established in 1867 it's one of the oldest tennis clubs in Wales. With its lawn and all-weather courts plus a club house with a bar it was made to measure for a keen sportsman to join, play tennis, meet new friends and generally get into the local scene. In my late 20's it was perfect to have such a facility on the doorstep. Turning up initially in a football shirt and yellow socks I was pulled aside by one of the older members and told that kit should be predominantly white. That was me put straight then. An immediate trip to the sports shop saw me wearing the most up-to-date pristine white kit. I don't need telling twice.

Another early incident occurred at the bar. Most unusually because it never happened before or since, I involuntarily passed wind. It rocked the club. Silence fell apart from one chap who quite reasonably said "Charming". Trying to make light of my unintended and embarrassing situation I turned to face the chap with the words "I've just said all I have to say to you". Still silence and then a laugh I would get used to. In hysterics bellowing in laughter it was Pip Powell who said, "Come and have a pint with me you silly bugger".

Pip was a real character. He became a life long friend. He sang with a male voice choir. We travelled back to Newport for his 60th birthday some years ago. The singing was awesome and Pip's solo outstanding. He introduced me to Rogerstone Golf Club where we had many an enjoyable round before going back to the tennis club which was his and, during our few years in Newport, my base. He and a few other boys introduced me to Indian curry. The Friday night trip to the Kohinoor Indian Restaurant became a ritual. The Kohinoor is actually a large colourless diamond that was found near Guntur in Andhra Pradesh, India in the 13th century weighing 793 carats.

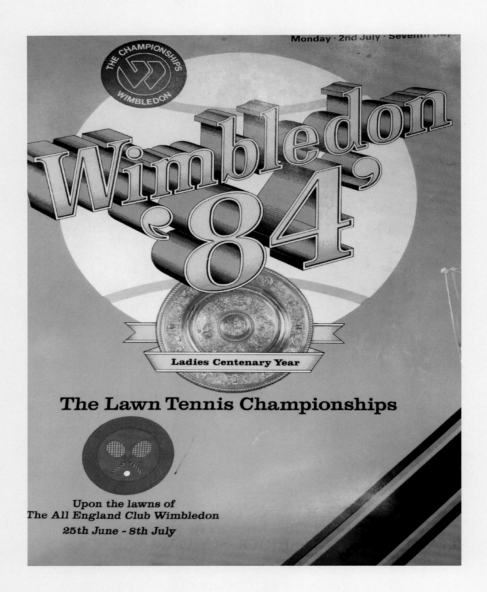

It originally was owned by the Kakatiya dynasty. Guess who owns it now. Think back to South Africa and Empire. Correct. Queen Elizabeth II in right of the crown. It's enough to get on your Elgin Marbles! Anyway, this restaurant was a diamond.

On Friday night especially, you could not just walk in. A knock on the door was required and a grill would slide open, so the owner could decide if you were worthy of entry i.e. not totally pissed and potentially trouble. We were given VIP treatment as one of our group was a top solicitor who had successfully defended the staff after one such customer was given a pasting while being thrown out. It was always a few pints at the club before going into town.

Pip and I kept in touch for 35 years. We had a £1 bet every time Wales played England. A £1 coin would be posted to Newport or Teignmouth. Last time he peculiarly sent £5 saying to have a pint on him. Just a few months ago on the eve of the latest game I rang to get his score prediction. His wife answered the phone sadly to say he had died. "When?" I asked her. "Ten minutes ago" said Jean. What a shaker that was. I will always remember Pip's friendship and his laugh. Not least the time Pip and Jean came to see us in Teignmouth. We drove to Dawlish to pick up a Chinese takeaway. We got the takeaway and got to the car, started to pull away only to hear a tap, tap on the window and a Chinese gentleman shouting "You no pay! you no pay!".

Somehow, and it was busy in there that night, Pip presumed I'd paid and vice versa. We stopped and paid before driving back with Pip now in hysterics with that laugh of his and the immortal words "Godwin, you really are a prat!".

I will also be grateful for all those halfway line debenture seat tickets he gave me to see Wales play rugby at the Arms Park. Pip being claustrophobic did not like crowds. The family debenture, England, Scotland, Ireland you name them, I was there courtesy of Pip. A kind and warm gentleman.

Stow Park had some fine tennis players and local rivals included Bridgend complete with JPR Williams, the Welsh rugby international and British Lions star who was a former Junior Wimbledon champion.

Stow Park introduced us to Wimbledon. They got an allocation of tickets, so we found ourselves on Centre Court a few times. Steffi Graf was unbelievable. She seemed to glide over the court and went on to win Wimbledon 7 times. John McEnroe, such a well-mannered boy and no, I cannot be serious, would serve and sprint amazingly fast to the net and a volley. Remarkable. Strawberries and Champagne. Hoards of people. A unique atmosphere. Centre Court was not covered in those days, so we were grateful for sunny days without rain interruptions or washouts.

Moving to Devon the tennis dropped off for a few years until I stumbled on a local tennis club at Trinity School. Within that club there was a group who played doubles on a Wednesday evening. Perfect. Competitive, reasonable standard. A couple of hours with floodlights if needed. An indoor facility if it rained. A drink and snacks afterwards. The added bonus of being with friendly, witty and nice people. Plenty of character and fun with some spicy debates on matters of the day. I raise my glass to Avril, Mikey, Marie, Chris, Mark, Gordon, Julian, Lorrie, Ancilla, David, Annie, Steve, Lorna and John L. All wonderful sporty people. Time and injuries, knees, hips and wrists have caught up on Wednesday nights but it was great for many years. Time for a pint

Chapter 37

SPORTING QUICKIES

PAOLA DI CANIO

The footballer from Rome played for Lazio, Juventus and was a cult hero at West Ham. He scored one of the goals of the century for them and on the other side of the coin got a long ban for man handling a referee and pushing him to the ground. Naughty boy with a temper in 2011 he became Swindon Town manager. He was a colourful value for money. A friend of mine moved his season ticket just so that he could sit in the stand behind the manager down on the touchline. After one Swindon goal he ran on to celebrate with the players as they raced to congratulate the goal scorer. He said when interviewed on Wiltshire radio "We are in big trouble. When I ran on I overtook my centre forward".

PETER ALLIS

I met him in Newport at a Ford Motor dealership road show. I asked him who were his personal favourite players. Nicklaus, Player and Trevino. It's no coincidence that the best commentators played the game themselves. Peter, now the voice of British Golf, won 20 tournaments including 3 British PGA championships, 5 top ten finishes in the Open as well as playing in 8 Ryder Cups. His father, Percy, was also a Ryder Cup player. It's in the genes.

DAVID HEMMERY

Olympic Gold Medal runner. Spotted him running around Marlborough. Out for a jog while teaching at Marlborough College. Looked surreal.

JOHN ALDRIDGE

We were having a meal in Praia de Luz, Portugal. John and his wife came in and took a nearby table. It took me back maybe twenty years to our Newport days. Newport County in their gold shirts had a fair team. John and his co-striker Tommy Tynan of Plymouth Argyle fame made a great partnership. From 1979-1984 John scored 70 goals in 170 appearances. I wanted to ask if he did anything after Newport! For the record he had a cracking career scoring 363 goals in 673 games for a number of clubs in particular 50 goals in 83 appearances for Liverpool. It would be unkind to mention his Cup Final penalty miss especially as it made him the first man to have a penalty kick saved in a Wembley FA Cup Final. Underdogs Wimbledon won 1-0 in 1988 and Dave Beasant saved the penalty. John was a crowd favourite at all his clubs and made 69 appearances for the Republic of Ireland with 19 goals.

IAN RUSH

Now Ian is Liverpool's all-time record goal scorer with 346 in 660 appearances. An all-time great player. He scored a record 28 goals for Wales in 73 games, 5 First Division (now Premiership) titles, 3 FA Cups, 5 League Cups and 2 European Cups. Stunning.

He wanted a 'no photos' at a party near Praia de Luz. It was just a social evening and my sister Rebecca, who lived nearby for a number of years, was there complete with friends and a camera as normal. "What do you mean, no photos?" "Who are you?" "I'm Ian Rush", "So?" "What do you do anyway?" Not a football fan our Rebecca!

RONNIE CORBETT

Playing in a pro-am at Stoke Poges. Now he really was short but always out for a laugh this national treasure kept a really small club in his bag for the crowd. A nice prop and the crowd loved it.

JASPER CARROT

At the same event making the gallery laugh with trademark mannerisms. Why do crowds line the fairways so close to the tees at pro-ams? The celebrities are not professional golfers. They can shank or hook off the tee just like you or me. Stand back!!

IAN BOTHAM

One of many clapping him through Babbacombe near Torquay on one of his many charity runs. Fast jog or walk and stops for no-one. Once on the move keep out of his way. He is on a mission and cannot stop because he would lose time and more importantly rhythm. Keep going Beefy.

LEN COLDWELL

The routine most nights when driving home from the office was to pop into the golf club for a quick pint. Driving right past it made it all too tempting. The usual like-minded boys would be in and one of them often was Len. Then a brewery representative he was good company. Normally sat at the bar he had bow legs which needed surgery. A good golfer like his son Gary, Len had got his bow-legged walk by playing cricket including for England in 7 tests taking 22 wickets with a best of 6 for 85 runs. He would have played more if not for Freddie Trueman and Brian Statham! With his bowling partner, Jack Flavell, Len was the main man when Worcestershire won for the first time the County Championship in 1964 and then again in 1965. He took 1076 first class wickets in 310 matches with a career best of 8 for 38 runs.

Just two other quick ones. He of course had a mutual respect for Freddie Trueman and enjoyed Freddie's quote on returning from a tour of India and the almost guaranteed 'Delhi Belly' trots. "It was 6 months before I could fart with any confidence!". One of the perils of overseas touring.

Len struggled with his legs. After one big operation and in recovery he entered a club competition. He won it! How good was that!

NIGEL MANSELL

Nigel Mansell owned and lived at Woodbury Park Golf Club. He came over to Teignmouth for a quiet game one day. Just him and his caddy. I walked along for a few holes and boy did he take care with every shot. His concentration was obvious right down to meticulous lining up of his putts even getting down to the green surface to be as sure as he could be reading the green. You don't get to be a great Formula One World Champion without absolute one minded concentration.

GARY PLAYER

Moving on from Nigel Mansell it was a treat indeed to go to his Woodbury Park Golf Club for a Nigel Mansell Seniors Tournament. He was trying at every opportunity to promote the club. His friend, Greg Norman, had his own locker complete with brass name plate. Nigel's trophy room was brilliant complete with his memorabilia and even the ring Paul Newman gave him around the time he was winning in America at the Indy 500.

Gary Player was the star name that day. "The harder I practice, the luckier I get". An all-time great winner of 9 majors made up of 3 Masters, 1 US Open, 3 Open Championships and 2 PGA Championships. This World famous small South African has logged over 15 million miles in travel. More than any athlete. His fitness defies logic and his amazing efforts to keep going are the stuff of legend.

He gave a little cameo sports warm-up class before going out to play. I walked the course with him and maybe half a dozen others. Can you believe that. A chance to walk with the Master and Devon was asleep. Unlucky boys and girls. He went around circa par on a course he had not played on before as far as I know. His concentration when over the ball was sterling. He did not commit to a shot until he was sure of what he wanted to do. In trouble on one hole he took numerous practice swings to get the feel right. To this day I wonder why so few were there. Maybe the publicity had not got into gear. A legend had turned up and it was a privilege to walk the course with him.

SANDY LYLE

"Why are you not resting Sandy?" I asked in a crowded tented village a few hours before he was due to tee off in the British Open. The US Masters champion explained that this worked for him. He did not want to be stuck in a hotel room but preferred to get into the atmosphere before going on to his practice routine. Whatever works, some logic in that.

SAM TORRENCE

Ryder Cup legend. Benson and Hedges. St Mellion Golf Club. Cold, wet and windy. Sam is waiting to tee off with a cigarette in his hand. He looks fed up. Our eyes met and I kind of looked at the weather and shrugged my shoulders. He looked and shook his head. No words necessary then.

JOHN SHEPHERD

"You must be loaded man" he said. I was talking to John, the West Indian Test cricketer at an NSPCC charity golf day at Teignmouth. We were talking about Barbados, his home island, that Anne and I were about to visit. He asked where we were staying and that was his response when I told him The Fairmont Royal Pavilions Hotel. John is a regular supporter of the charity day, guest of our mutual friend Adrian Whittle. Adrian lived at one time next to Dave Thomas, the ex-England football winger and gets a mention in his book. He smokes a pipe when playing golf. We are waiting for his trousers to catch fire as he pops the pipe away.

John and Adrian are good buddies and Adrian tells the story of when he played golf with John and the great Sir Vivian Richards. It was dusk and getting too dark to play. Viv commented "This is crazy John, all I can see is Adrian and your eyes!"

Chapter 38

IT'S THE WAY I TELL THEM

FRANK CARSON. (IRISH COMEDIAN)

We were outside the Princess Theatre Torquay as Frank arrived for his evening show. At the same time a bus full of OAP ladies were getting off their bus.

"Be Jesus" shouted Frank to the old dears "No-one told me this was a Miss World competition". "It's the way I tell them". He had them laughing even before they got into the theatre.

Come the interval I was at the bar there. The phone rang. It was Frank. The barman called his colleague over "Quick as you can, Mr Carson wants a pint of lager and he wants it now!"

WARREN MITCHELL (ALF GARNETT), ACKER BILK AND FRANK CARSON

All three appeared at the C&T Harris Woodlands Social Club in Calne. Dad was Chairman of the club. At the end of each show he would invite the star to come and have a drink with him and his family. I was in my late teens then, maybe early twenties. Dad would send a car just down the road for a selection of food produce as a little gift for the star to take away compliments of the firm.

After a drink and a laugh, it was quite a sight to see Acker Bilk walk out with a pound of sausages in his hand or 'Alf Garnett' with a couple of pork pies! Acker's 'Stranger on the Shore' was a huge hit. In the charts for over 50 weeks and No.1 in the USA. I can still remember as he played it on his clarinet.

PRICKED IN PENINA

We enjoy Henry Cotton's Penina. If you go there try Cactos Restaurant just down the road a few hundred yards. Try and play Palmeros Golf Course also. Good fun.

Sir Henry won the British Open 3 times and his taste for the good life is reflected in the high standards at Penina. We had a 50th Birthday trip here but I just want to touch on an occurrence during a later trip. We were playing with an Irish couple. My ball went behind a bush and I tried to play it out. My glove was seeping blood and in pain I took it off to see a thorn had gone clear through my middle finger.

Rushing back to the clubhouse holding my finger up in what could have been thought to be an obscene gesture, the buggy raced along. On one tee the players were about to tee off. Anne asked if she should stop. Not likely, this was a medical emergency. I do hope no-one was offended as we went through the course with one finger in the air.

The resident medical man was great. He was back from Afghanistan where he was a medical assistant. He had seen worse than a thorn. He took care removing the thorn explaining that if it snapped it was a hospital job. It came out, so it was back to our Irish friends, missing just one par 5. They were surprised to see us back at all but as I explained, we did not win two World wars without a bit of backbone! Besides, with the cost of a round at Penina how could you not return to the course!

HOLD ON TO YOUR KIT BAG

Playing football in Newport was never easy. It seemed to rain most weeks and a water-logged pitch was common. In order to avoid a fixture backlog Christchurch FC, who I was turning out for, had a plan B. There was a flat, not used very much and well drained pitch just outside Newport a few miles from our home ground. The only problem was that it was part of the grounds of the local mental asylum which by its nature housed people in need of help and care.

Arriving for one game a young chap said hello, and could he carry my kit bag to the changing room. Wanting to humour him I said "Sure, of course". Big mistake. Before you could blink he was off. He legged it with my kit bag like an Olympic sprinter into the main building! Twenty minutes to kick off and no football boots was not ideal preparation. Luckily one of the attendant male nurses knew the patient and tracked him down.

During the game another inmate decided to run onto the pitch to feign injury. He was copying a player and wanted the trainer on. Good job the referee did not book him. He was known as 'Napoleon'.

In South Wales, it was all about rugby and tennis. The footballing days were closing.

Jensen, our eldest grandson, was around four when we took him to Paignton Zoo. He enjoyed looking at all the animals. Standing at the front of a crowd of tourists and holiday makers looking at the giraffes he brought the house down when he shouted loudly, "Grampy, when can we see the dinosaurs?"

Jacqueline, our eldest daughter, when around the same age made a couple of sandcastles on a fairly deserted and large beach. When asked whey she had stopped after making two she replied "Well, it's only fair. I want to leave enough sand for all the other boys and girls!"

I normally do the driving. One exception occurred in Ibiza. Anne, who is a good driver, was behind the wheel. It had not rained for weeks but chose to on this particular day. The road became slippery and treacherous, more than we realised. Anne braked on a bend and lost it. We shot across the road between a bus and a car spinning around before stopping. Time had stood still. A lucky escape.

I don't recall exactly what was said but let your imagination take care of that. Anne closed the dialogue with the classic comment, "Well, if you don't like my driving you can drive yourself next time!"

Chapter 39

YOU ARE HAVING A LAUGH

My wife has been trying on some of her old clothes to see if they still fit. "Eureka" she shouted and proudly walked in – wearing a scarf!

A husband arrived home to find his wife lying naked on the bed "What's this all about?" he asked. Well, I've no clothes. You never buy me clothes". He opened her wardrobe and said "Look, you have this red dress, you have this yellow dress, this pink dress, "Hello Bert!", "this blue dress…

A Jehovah Witness knocks on a door. The man says, "Come in, you are welcome. It's cold out. Sit in my chair by the fire. Would you like tea, a chocolate cake? Now, what do you want?" The Jehovah says, "I don't know, I've never got this far before!"

Prince Charles is being interviewed on TV in Newcastle wearing a ridiculous fox's hat. Excuse me sir, said the interviewer. Why are you wearing the fox's that? Prince Charles burst into tears. "It's mummy's fault, I told her I was going to Newcastle". She said, "Where the fox's that!!"

Ken Dodd in Torquay at the Princess Theatre. He was 88 then but what a legend. A man went into an outdoor activity shop. He was going duck shooting and wanted a camouflage suit. He walked around the store a few times before calling the manager. "Look here, he said. I've been looking around the store but cannot find your camouflage suits". "Yes", said the Manager. "They are good, aren't they?!"

Lord Sebastian Coe, Olympic gold medal winner in the 1500 metres and one of our greatest ever runners presented his ticket to the steward at Chelsea Football Club. "Sorry sir, but you cannot come in here. Your entrance is on the other side of the ground". "For goodness sake man its five minutes to kick-off" "Don't you recognize me? I'm Sebastian Coe, one of the Country's fastest ever runners". "Well sir, if you are as fast as you say you are you won't miss the kick-off, will you?!"

A man talking to his wife in bed. "You know I'll never get over you darling". "Well you'll just have to walk around me then".

Tommy Cooper being introduced to the Queen after a Royal Variety Show. "Do you like football Ma'am?" "Not really" said the Queen. "Can I have your cup final tickets then?!!"

A guy was at a clinic for a sperm test. He was given a container and a copy of Playboy. While being shown to his empty cubicle he could not help seeing another guy with a container going into his cubicle with a rather attractive nurse who shut the door. "I say" he asked. "Why the different treatment?" "Easy" said the nurse. "He's in BUPA!"

A Scotsman gently taking a fly from his whisky, holding it over the glass he says while shaking it "Spit it out!"

A member had his ashes scattered on the course. Rather like many of his shots, they were blown out of bounds.

Guinness Book of Records. Chairman proposes 3 nominees

1) Smallest Person – Tom Thumb – Agreed

2) Prettiest Person – Cinderella – Agreed

3) Ugliest Person – Quasimodo – Not Agreed.

Disappointed he says "Well, who's Jeremy Clarkson?!"

Press set up the ambassador with sly "What would you like for Christmas?" question.

French Ambassador – I want World peace

USA Ambassador – I want an end to war

English Ambassador – A potted plant would be nice.

Sex and golf – two things you can enjoy without being good at it.

Equality. A woman looks over her garden wall to see a man in the garden nude. She reports him and he is fined as a pervert for indecent exposure. A man looks over the hedge to see a lady in the nude sun bathing. He is fined for being a peeping Tom!

A greenkeeper was sent to the doctor by his wife after 10 years with no children. A scruffy sort of chap he came home dressed in a pin stripe suit, bowler hat and a Financial Times under his arm. "The Doctor said I was impotent. I figure if I am impotent I should dress like someone special!

Two Seniors playing golf "Watch my ball Harry, my eyesight is going". "Did you see it? Where did it go?" "Yes, but I've forgotten!"

> A man suspects his wife may be dead. Sex is still the same, but the ironing is building up.

A widow talked to the urn containing her husband's ashes which was kept on the mantlepiece. She said "Jack, I hope you understand but I've met someone else. He has bought me the jewellery you could not afford. He has bought me the fur coat you could not afford. He has booked the holiday you could not afford." She then proceeded to tip the ashes out on to the table before saying "Now, about that blow job you always wanted and I never gave you!"

Paddy was pleased to make love for 1 hour 3 minutes. Not so pleased when he realised the clocks had gone forward an hour.

A Scotsman was cleared of raping a cat. The Judge was insistent that in all his years he had never seen a Scotsman put anything in the kitty.

A golfer gets aroused while having a sports massage. The lady says, "Do you need hand relief?" He says that would be nice, so she says "Okay, I'll go and make a cup of tea. Shout when you are finished".

Watching rugby at Kingsholm Gloucester. With the players getting stuck in at a ruck a rather big fan was heard to say just behind us "Give him a good kicking". His mate said, "That's no way for a policeman to talk".

The Antiques Roadshow was coming to town and locals were urged to look in their attics for old valuables. One guy turned up with quite a large looking heavy specimen. Our expert looked it over before telling our disappointed local, "I'm sorry sir, but it's worth f**k all, you have brought in your water tank!".

An Australian guy goes into a bar in the Greek Islands. Jill, the Australian barmaid, takes his order and notices his Australian accent. Over the course of the night they talk quite a bit. At the end of the night he asks her if she wants to have sex with him. Although she is attracted to him she says no. He then offers to pay her £200 for the deed. Jill is travelling the world and because she is short of funds, she agrees. The next night the guy turns up again and after showing her plenty of attention throughout the night he asks if she will sleep with him again for £200. She figures, in for a penny in for a pound – and it was fantastic the night before – so she agrees. This goes on for 5 nights. On the sixth night the guy comes into the bar. But this night he orders a beer and just goes and sits in the corner. Jill is disappointed and thinks that maybe she should pay him more attention. She goes over and sits next to him. She asks him where he is from and he tells her Melbourne. "So am I", she says. "What suburb in Melbourne?" "Glen Iris" he says. "That's amazing" she says, "So am I – what street?" "Cameo Street" he says. "This is unbelievable" she says, "What number?" He says, "number 20" and she is astonished. "You are not going to believe this" she says, "I'm from number 22 and my parents still live there!" "I know" he says, "your father gave me £1000 to give you!"

I asked my secretary why she had stopped answering the phone. "It's a waste of time" she said. "Nearly all the calls are for you".

184

Do not forget the chap who sat at the bar in his local all night and got hammered. At closing time he got off his bar stool and fell to the floor. No matter how hard he tried to get up, he could not. He crawled out of the pub and a taxi driver got him into a cab and drove him home. He fell out of the taxi. The next day his wife told him he was drunk last night and should be ashamed. "Rubbish", he cried. "I may have had a couple, that's all". "You were drunk, and I can prove it" she said. "The landlord has phoned to confirm you were wasted and completely gone. He also wants you to go to the pub this morning. He wants you to collect your wheel chair which you forgot last night!"

Paddy on a train. He said to the man opposite, "Excuse me. Are you reading that paper you are sat on?".

A prostitute told Paddy she would do anything for £250. "It's a deal" said Paddy. "Would you go and paint my house!"

Paddy was thrilled to finish his jigsaw in 3 months. It said 3-5 years on the box!

Talking to a Welsh lady, Paddy said "Two great things come out of Wales. Brilliant rugby players and beautiful women. "What position do you play love?".

"Three Irishmen decided to trick their way into the Olympics. The first one picked up a manhole cover and got in saying he was in the discus. The second one got in with a spear saying javelin. Paddy failed with holding a roll of barbed wire saying "Fencing"

Chapter 40

OTHER SPORTS

HORSE RACING

Love the spectacle, the colours and seeing the horses in full flight. Go to the races rarely but always enjoy it. Went to the Derby one year. Missed the first few races due to the crowds and our old bus taking too long to arrive. Stood by the winning post and found out it's not the place to stand for a decent view. Had £5 on Mill Reef who won the Derby. The odds were 3-1. Saw a few horses' heads flash past.

My sister Rebecca

Betting is a mugs game but when you do win, it's a thrill. Some of the race results are dubious. You know the horse that has looked like a donkey in previous races and then comes in at 75-1. Is someone having a laugh along the way?

My best bet was 66-1 British Open at St Andrews. Thank you, John Daly. Well, he had played well there before and was off the juice!

My worst bet. No comment. 5th Amendment.

My sister is a natural with horses. Apparently, they sense if you are at ease in the saddle. Well, I'm not. Best to leave them alone then as proved when Rebecca visited and I fixed her up for a ride. I went along but the horse I was given was so big I pulled out. Just as well, because the guy who took my place was thrown off in the first field. Trust your instincts boys and girls!

BOXING

When the bell rings you are on your own. The closest I got to the ring apart from a schoolboy boxing club was presenting a prize at a Lloyds and Scottish Finance sponsored tournament. I've been to plenty of fights and while there are risks it also brings opportunity in some cases to literally get out of the ghetto. We have had some great fights and fighters over the years. Lennox Lewis in my time may have been the best UK boxer. His hero was Mohammed Ali. What a star.

Let's not forget Joe Calzaghe. 46 fights, 46 wins. You cannot argue with that. He held his super-middleweight WBO titles for over 10 years and 21 defences. Crackerjack.

We had a day out a few years ago. Aston Villa v Everton in the afternoon then up to Manchester to see Chris Eubank defeat Henry Wharton. Classic atmosphere and a masterclass from Eubank. Boys need a day out now and again. So do the girls.

My earliest memory of boxing was sparring as a young boy with my brother Gary. My father bought us proper gloves. He thought it important we could look after ourselves and each other. We were shown how to keep up a good guard, to jab and then bring over a good right hand. He taught us to watch the opponent's eyes. I had to be careful being the eldest and three years older. If I hit Gary too hard then the old man would hit me. All part of a well-rounded upbringing!

ATHLETICS

Total respect for the dedication and training. They talk of the loneliness of the long-distance runner. Going through the pain barrier. I love the middle-distance races and hark back to Coe, Ovett and Cram. Usain Bolt has been an all-time legend. The fastest human ever timed. I mean, 3 golds at 3 Olympics. One hundred metres, two hundred metres and 4x100 metres relay. China, England and Brazil. He will win gold anywhere! They need to sort the illegal performances drugs out. It's coming up all the time, which leads me on to

CYCLING

Well, we watched the Tour of Britain cycle through Teignmouth. Not overly exciting really. The biggest cheer was for an old chap who went past just before the road was cleared. He looked like he was off to his allotment on his bike and seemed confused at all the clapping. Priceless.

We watch the Sky Team train in Tenerife in winter. Respect for the speed up and down the mountain roads. The bicycles are expensive bits of kit. Lance Armstrong put a shadow over the sport. I mean, 7 consecutive Tour de France wins before being stripped for doping. Really!

DARTS

There was a time when this was a bit of fun down your local. Beer bellied guys swigging back pints. Not a proper sport. Eric Bristow lifted the profile and of course Phil Taylor has dominated for years. With TV big crowds I would say now it is a sport given the high level of skill required to get to the top. When players step up to the Oche they need to bring their A game. You need to be able to add and subtract quickly too. It helps if you know which number on the board to go for!

FISHING

Just support your local fishmonger. It's so popular I must be missing something for sure. Just not one for me.

RUGBY UNION

I played full back and could take penalties and conversions. However, playing for Calne Bentley Grammar I called for a mark. A fifteen stone brute of a forward ignored it and smashed my legs together before collapsing on top of me. At that point I was in no doubt that football would stay as my preferred option. I like to go and see our local team at Teignmouth. My allegiances are now with the outstanding Exeter Chiefs and I watch all the Internationals. A great sport maybe with too many obscure rules and too much time out for TV reviews. Keep the game moving please.

BULL FIGHTING

Diabolical. Dubious to call it a sport. I went to one 40 years ago with brother Gary. Barbaric. We walked out. Bulls weakened with lances, horses gored by bulls, a baying crowd. The Matador closes for the kill which is not always clean. The carcass dragged away to the waiting butchers under the stand. The bull meat can be back at the hotel before you are. Colour and spectacle, yes. Tradition, yes. A sport, no chance.

WINTER SPORT

Loved by those who ski. Why do so many return with broken bones? Why do ice-skating rinks have little pools of blood all over? Leave it to Torville and Dean or John Curry me thinks. On holiday in Italy we did climb to the top of an Eddie the Eagle Olympic ski jump and look down. Madness!

WRESTLING

Pantomime time.

Chapter 41

UPRISING CHIEFS

Saturday, May 27th, 2017. We are walking on the road 50 yards from the main entrance to Twickenham. Crowds lined the route and thronged around the huge iron main gates. The fans began to cheer and clap, waving flags with great excitement. What a welcome as Paul, Cameron and I waved in appreciation. Hold it! After a few seconds we looked behind to see the Exeter Chiefs team bus five yards behind us! Never mind get off the bus, this was a case of getting out of the way of the bus! We still laugh about it.

Exeter Chiefs were at the home of English Rugby to play the Wasps in the final for the English Rugby Union Trophy. The Championship Final.

The semi-final had produced a last-minute victory over Saracens 18-16 to put out the reigning English and European champions. Behind with seconds left, Henry Slade fired an inspirational free kick to within a few yards of the Wasps try line. From the line out, the Chiefs drove over for Teignmouth's very own Sam Simmonds to score the winning try. Unbelievable. I have rarely experienced such emotion. The crowd made the most amazing sound. You could almost touch the atmosphere. A six foot plus bear of a man stood next to me burst into tears! "I don't care" he said, "I am just so happy". Time for a pint then.

The final saw things all square 20-20 after normal time. Two tries, two conversions and two penalties for each team. Twenty minutes of extra time. The Chiefs won it when Gareth Steenson, our Mr Reliable, kicked a penalty. Nerves of steel under such pressure. 23-20 and Champions!

The rise of Exeter Chiefs in recent times has been a truly remarkable fairy tale. A sporting achievement as unlikely as Swindon Town winning the League cup in 1969 or Leicester City winning the Premiership in 2016.

Founded in 1871, the club played mainly in Devon. One claim to fame came in 1905 when Exeter Rugby Club hosted the first match played by the New Zealand National Rugby Union team on English soil at the County Ground between New Zealand and the Devon County XV. From that game New Zealand became known as the 'All Blacks'. And not many people know that!

In the 1990's the club turned semi-professional. They also changed their name to Exeter Chiefs as they had been known in the 1930's. In 1997 they were promoted to the Premiership Two from the National League One. Back in the County Ground days a few hundred people would turn up and you could even drive your car into the ground and park near to the pitch. Mind you, it meant you were taking a chance on a rugby ball landing on your bonnet and doing some damage!

In 2006 the Chiefs moved to their magnificent new stadium purpose built at Sandy Park near the M5 complete with conference and banqueting facilities. After near misses, promotion to the top tier came in 2009. Winning the Championship in 2017 meant Exeter are the only club to win the top three tiers of English Rugby. They have also won the Anglo-Welsh Cup twice. They have progressed year by year and currently sit top of the tree as champions with a great squad and a 12,500-seat stadium regularly sold out. The fans chant the Tomahawk Chop is now recognized all around the Country. Mutants from somewhere or other in 2016 asked the Chiefs to change their name as it could be offensive appropriation of Native American culture. Has the World gone mad?

It has been a privilege and joy to have been able to enjoy the ride. This is a club to be proud of. A solid foundation built by Tony Rowe OBE and his fellow Directors has enabled the playing side to grow under Rob Baxter, Director of Rugby. A youth policy has produced players such as Henry Slade, Sam Simmonds, Luke Cowan-Dickie and Jack Nowell all of whom have come through the academy and developed into great players with the first team. They have all now as young men been selected for England.

Players such as Geoff Parling and Thomas Waldron have joined the Chiefs to pass on their experience as top players nearing the end of their careers but determined to make the most of another opportunity. Dean Mumm, the Australian International, came over to Captain the side and what a contact. Back in Australia he has introduced several good Aussies to the Chiefs.

Recruitment all round is outstanding. And here's the thing. Players want to come to Exeter. They can see the product, the results, and spirit. Who would not want to be a part of it? These are proper men. Hard men. Skillful men. They have an intensity which I have rarely seen in sport. The David Lloyd Leisure and Tennis Club sits next to the ground. When I go for a little work out I regularly see the players who drop in after training. Don't mess with these boys. Just walking past the likes of Don Armand or Dave Ewers you can see what big powerful guys they are. Dave was out injured so I asked him when he would be back. He looked at me with a look that would halt the Terminator and said, "I am back". No problem Dave, I am on your side. Tackling these guys is beyond belief. What a club! What a future!

Chapter 42

SEE YOU LATER – GRAND SPORTS DINNER

Who shall we invite? Well, friends and family of course, but we need sporting heroes to grace the occasion.

Representing **FOOTBALL**, I want Don Rogers and John Trollope. They worked well together for Swindon Town and are still buddies. Don, you may have picked up was the best player I saw and John the most loyal of men. His MBE for record appearances is testament to that. Jimmy Greaves, our greatest goal scorer, has to be there. Brother Gary would be table host and represent Calne Town!

CRICKET would see David Gower OBE, ace batsman, tiger moth pilot and gentleman. As a renowned wine connoisseur, he naturally selects the wine. Sir Ian Botham, our greatest all rounder and Knight of the Realm is a must. Beefy would be good company. Marcus Trescothick MBE scored plenty for Somerset and England, so he could pop down from Taunton. Table hosts would be John Davis, my old cricketing chum and Daniel Slade, my cousin who shares my passion for sport and cricket in particular in his case.

RUGBY UNION next. Jonny Wilkinson CBE. World Cup hero. England's finest. Sir Gareth Edwards, one of the greats. Rob Baxter, Exeter Chiefs Director of Rugby and miracle worker. Table host, whoever is Captain at Teignmouth Golf Club at the time as the club would be the venue and that would be polite!

GOLF well it's got to be Sir Nick Faldo, the best British golfer ever. Also invited, Tony Jacklin CBE, winner of two major championships and European Ryder Cup hero. Let's also invite Ian Woosnam OBE, 1991 Masters Champion. He knows how to party and what a character. Table host, Richard Armitage, 'Armo'. He would give as good as he gets!

TENNIS would be represented by Sir Andy Murray, two times Wimbledon, US Open and Olympic Champion. Sue Barker OBE is a local girl from Paignton. French Open Champion in 1976 and after tennis a top BBC sports presenter notably at Wimbledon and A Question of Sport. Table host would be my wife Anne as it's her favourite programme. Tim Henman OBE also gets an invite for contribution to tennis over the years. Six grand slam semi-finals with no cigar!

SNOOKER. Local World Champion Ray Reardon MBE and the legendary grinder Steve Davis OBE also a multi-World Champion. Both the best of their era. Let's throw in another World Champion Ronnie O'Sullivan OBE on his day pure magic. Table host, Nick Hunt, in honour of our Thursday night snooker sessions!

MOTOR RACING. Jenson Button MBE, World Champion, and I knew your Dad son. Nigel Mansell CBE, World Champion and memories of Woodbury! Lewis Hamilton MBE, current top gun and World Champion. Table host, my old mate Flash because he has always loved his cars!

Other guests would include Lord Sebastian Coe for athletics, Lennox Lewis CBE for boxing, Sir A P McCoy and Lester Piggott for horse racing. You will note Lester has no honour after his name. His OBE was withdrawn after a tax evasion conviction. Many of us were surprised at this given his popularity and sterling career. Sir Peter O'Sullivan, the star commentator, even took it up with the Queen at a luncheon opportunity on behalf of his friend Lester. "Ma'am, admittedly he nourished the treasury below the level of requirement but," and then he went into the mitigating circumstances. The Queen put her knife and fork down and said "I like the way you put it, but he was rather naughty you know, He was not only rather naughty but he was rather stupid because he paid his tax bill on a bank that had not come up in the case and had not been investigated". In other words, it was one thing to avoid tax but quite another to be thick with one's defence!

Celebrity trials always attract attention. Look at Ken Dodd. No Liverpool jury was going to find him guilty of tax evasion. He was a hero in his home city. Besides, as he always said, "Tax used to be a penny in the pound and I thought it still was!"

Jimmy Tarbuck, the comedian, was found guilty of driving over the drink limit. Before sentence the Judge asked him if he had anything to say. "Yes, your honour. Can I have a lift home!"

A sports dinner is a nice way to finish while sport of course never does. It is always a work in progress. Each year brings new champions, seasons, fixtures and excitement. That's why we love sport.

As I conclude, this will be a busy week. A visit to see Somerset tomorrow. Two rounds of golf later in the week. Exeter Chiefs have reached another Twickenham final. Anne has booked a Baltic cruise and our tickets have arrived for a Rolling Stones concert in Cardiff.

ROCK ON!

CHEERS!

My mother Desna, a wonderful inspiration to us, carries a card in her handbag. It simply states – 'A day without a laugh is a day wasted'. I also relate to a Paul McCartney lyric – 'Heaven does not only wait for those who congregate', spot on.

I finish with a photograph of Jacqueline and Fiona preparing to fly from Exeter Airport for a business meeting.

Cheers!